ISP

SOME
OF MY
BEST
FRIENDS

ESSAYS ON LIP SERVICE

TAJJA ISEN

ONE SIGNAL
PUBLISHERS
———
ATRIA

NEW YORK   LONDON   TORONTO   SYDNEY   NEW DELHI

**ONE SIGNAL
PUBLISHERS**

ATRIA

An Imprint of Simon & Schuster, Inc.
1230 Avenue of the Americas
New York, NY 10020

First One Signal Publishers/Atria Books hardcover edition April 2022

ONE SIGNAL PUBLISHERS / ATRIA BOOKS and colophon are
trademarks of Simon & Schuster, Inc.

For information about special discounts for bulk purchases, please contact Simon &
Schuster Special Sales at 1-866-506-1949 or business@simonandschuster.com.

The Simon & Schuster Speakers Bureau can bring authors to your live event. For
more information or to book an event, contact the Simon & Schuster Speakers
Bureau at 1-866-248-3049 or visit our website at www.simonspeakers.com.

Manufactured in the United States of America

1   3   5   7   9   10   8   6   4   2

Library of Congress Control Number: 2022930535

ISBN 978-1-9821-7842-0
ISBN 978-1-9821-7844-4 (ebook)

For my parents

Contents

Between me and the other world there is ever an unasked question: unasked by some through feelings of delicacy; by others through the difficulty of rightly framing it. All, nevertheless, flutter around it. They approach me in a half-hesitant sort of way, eye me curiously or compassionately and then, instead of saying directly, How does it feel to be a problem? they say, I know an excellent colored man in my town.

    —W.E.B. Du BOIS, *The Souls of Black Folk*, 1903

In 11 years working I have always been extremely inclusive without even trying to. My best friends are rappers my boyfriends have been rappers . . . Respect it.

    —LANA DEL REY, Instagram, 2021

Introduction

Near the end of the first *Toy Story* film, an uprising takes place. The familiar conceit of the plot is that toys are conscious. They can think and talk, feel and plot revenge. But no one is supposed to know: Every time a person walks into the room, the playthings flop to the ground, still and glassy-eyed and all *who, me?* about having free will. Their oppressor is a kid named Sid, who likes to take apart his store-bought toys and remake them into new ones. Seems harmless, maybe even anti-capitalist. But because Sid's creations involve dismembered dolls—and also because he has bad teeth, a skull T-shirt, and the basement pallor of an incel—we're meant to recognize that he's a creep. This is not a bright and curious child trying to minimize his carbon footprint. This is a sadist getting off on torture. The circumstances, the toys decide, are grave enough to break the cardinal rule and reveal their sentience.

Leading the revolt is our hero, Sheriff Woody. Sid has Buzz Lightyear, Woody's rival-turned-bro, strapped to a rocket. He's about to light the fuse when Woody stages a distraction, saying his action-figure lines though no one is pulling his string. Sid stops, frowns. The toy is all the way across the yard. The yard is empty. When he skulks over to Woody and picks him up, things turn personal: "That's right. I'm talking to you, Sid Phillips." Sid's face contorts in panic as the other shoe drops: He hasn't been making cool, alternative toys. He's been *butchering living creatures*. Woody, not one for subtlety, really drives this point home: "We don't like being blown up, Sid. Or smashed, or ripped apart." What happens next is straight out of a horror film, enough to terrify the kid I was in 1995. The army of toys closes in like they're about to rip *Sid* apart, mutilated dolls rising from muddy puddles and a sandbox, lurching with outstretched arms, crying *Mama*. The most iconic of Sid's experiments, a one-eyed baby's head on a crablike metal body, drops from the sky and caresses Sid's temples. This has already been pretty traumatic for the kid, but what truly breaks him is Woody's final demand: the sheriff rotates his head a cool 360 and says, in a voice that drips with threat, "So play . . . *nice*."

This scene is my favorite metaphor to describe what it's felt like, over the past several years, as corporations, public figures, and cultural industries became fluent in the language of social justice: a bunch of objects opening their mouths to declare a revolutionary conscious-ness. After this decade's uprisings against police violence, the wave of inclusion statements, high-profile hires, and higher-profile apolo-gies meant that too many *things* were suddenly talking. Entities that should not, in any rational view of the world, have been able to speak at all—candy brands, emojis, style guides, road surfaces, the *New York Times* bestseller list—were suddenly animate, alive. They stroked my temples and chucked me under the chin, vowing that a new order was on its way and, what's more, I was going to like it. Sometimes, the noisemaking led to changes in systems and policies that have made them more equitable. Mostly, the noise was an end in itself to prove its makers were in step with the times.

Not long after watching *Toy Story*, I became a voice actor, a job I've held for more than twenty years. When white celebrities swore off playing cartoon roles of color, our field was hit with public scrutiny. Animation was suddenly in the news, and reporters were especially keen to learn from racialized actors and our supposed vindication. I also work as a magazine editor, another field not known for being colorful. There too, as senior leadership professed their respect for Black lives despite all the counterevidence in what they'd published, I sensed heads swiveling in my direction. All of this felt unsettling. But none of it was new. Certain establishments have always said what they think the public wants to hear, whether for profit or cachet. The more I thought about it, the more I realized this dynamic is predominantly how I—and, I'd venture, most people—have long interacted with the institutions that shape my life: they let us down and we adapt; then they apologize for letting us down and promise to fix things; then they break their promises shortly afterward or never act on them at all. This book is about how we live, and what we demand, amid such token apologies and promises.

Some of these acts are easily knowable for what they are: progressive language thinly pasted over capitalism and white supremacy. Take the flexible use of the word *antiracism*, whose colloquial meaning has been diluted from "actively opposing violence" into a synonym for "being nice and buying stuff." Or elevating art by Black creators solely for what it says about trauma, but not for what it says about beauty or what it means to be alive. Or buttoning a racist comment with "some of my best friends are . . ." At other times, progressive language is closer to founding myth: the story a country tells itself about its moral superiority, or the law about its perfectibility, or white feminism about its vulnerability. Taken together, these acts coalesce into a distinctive force: the pull of our attention away from foundational cracks to point toward something prettier out the window. In these essays, I call that bait and switch "lip service." We know this move so well by now and have become grudging experts at spotting it. It's like the moment from 30 *Rock* when Steve Buscemi's private-eye character tries to blend in with a group of students by wearing a backwards cap and band tee and asks, "How do you do, fellow kids?" Nobody was ever going to buy that. This book zeroes in on that type of moment—of slangy speech so clearly at odds with a speaker's underlying aims—to explore how this dynamic has become such a big part of contemporary life, and how we might resist the world it tries to sell us.

When I was younger, I often found myself mistaking lip service for the real thing. The journey of this book, out of complacency and into demand, is also often my journey of exploring the contexts that have shaped and implicated me. The first essay in the collection is about entering the color-blind utopia that I (and much of the public) once imagined cartoons to be, and why we won't reach a more equitable industry by simply tweaking the casting process. The next is about my teenaged affair with the literary canon, growing up in a white suburb, and my failure to turn both of those things into an artistic practice. To round out the book's first cluster, I explore how the word *diversity* was defanged by a U.S. Supreme Court justice who feared the political left, and how that paved the way for the trope of the "diversity hire." By the next few essays, I'm less sanguine. I look at the personal-essay economy and white feminism, respectively, as separate but related systems that reward certain kinds of vulnerability as politically good. Then I explore the gap between word and action in the North American legal system, and how that first attracted and then repelled me from the law. The book ends by exploring several forms of resistance: the protest genre of the demand letter; recent calls for accountability in the publishing industry; and, finally, my own demands of Canada's national fictions, after those fictions have spent years demanding everything from me.

Every field I explore relies on its own kind of lip service to tell a story about moral rightness. How it plays out depends on the context, but what all of them share is the gulf between the scope of the problem and the inadequacy of the proposed solution. I've chosen *lip service* in lieu of other terms that might seem more obvious, like *performative allyship* or *virtue signaling*, both of which have grown too charged to use in good faith (and would sound bad in a subtitle). My hope, with *lip service*, is to suggest that sometimes these misguided acts and actors truly are sincere. I also value the term's implicit reminder that a well-meaning gesture might be all talk. *Some of My Best Friends* is interested in such gaps: between what we say and what we do; what we do and what we value; what we value and what we imagine to be possible.

But it's also about the comedy of it all. The predictable flops in the theater of good intentions; a thousand little laughs on the road to hell. The cliched joke about the token friend, and the ghost of the racist comment that precedes it, exemplify so many things that still get called progress: tokenization, representation, revisionism, guilt, catharsis. Not only does the punch line think it's solved the problem of inequality, it suggests there never *was* a problem to begin with—how could there have been, when we've always been best buddies? Even Sid from *Toy Story*, one imagines, would have said before they turned on him that some of his best friends were toys.

The world is full of chatty playthings desperate to play nice. I hope these essays help make sense of the noise.

Hearing Voices

In the early 2000s, the North American voice-over industry lowered its entry requirements. Icons of the nineties, like the *Rugrats* toddlers or the tweens from *Doug*, had been played by actors far beyond those ages. Being able to sound younger, or like anything you're not—animal, vegetable, mineral, conservative, ginger—has long been part of animation's magic. But as the millennium turned, trends changed. Producers started to hire actual kids. If the nineties sounded worldly, a little wry, then the coveted tone of the aughts was innocence. The authenticity boom had begun: *Young characters on an animated show*, the rule went, *should be played by young people*.

At nine years old, I was suddenly tall enough to ride the roller coaster. It was a good time to be young and fame-hungry, though I assumed my face would be the thing that got me on TV, not my voice. I loved to do impressions, but I considered them a practical skill, like doing the Heimlich or starting a fire with two sticks—sure, it can save your life, but it's not exactly the thing you plan to be known for. I mostly used my voice to manipulate people. When I dialed my dad's office and an assistant answered, I'd ask, in a British accent, for her to "put Dr. Isen on the line" if I wasn't in the mood for small talk. When family friends called and thought I was my mom, I didn't correct them right away, hoping they would spill juicier gossip. Other times, the stakes were higher: when talking to the white girls that filled my Toronto suburb, I'd emulate their upspeak to deflect from our more visible differences. The voice, I was learning, could be both play and power. When I told my parents I wanted to be an actor just as cartoons were becoming a kids' market, I found the perfect outlet—and probably dodged a future conviction for vocal fraud.

My first voice audition was for a reboot of *The Berenstain Bears*, the classic children's series about a bear family, whose name the internet regularly freaks out over the spelling of. The studio was in one of Toronto's former industrial neighborhoods, just beyond where the railway tracks start slicing off the city's western edge. Sitting in the waiting room with my dad, I felt the hum of collective anxiety, like a pediatrician's office full of better-dressed kids. Unlike auditions for on-camera projects, which involve pedantically detailed wardrobe suggestions, no one tells you what to wear to a cartoon casting call. Absent of any guidelines, several guardians had apparently assumed that "job interview" was the next-closest thing. I'd chosen my outfit myself: the orange turtleneck sweater, veined with glittering thread, which I'd worn in my professional headshot—the same headshot I clutched a printed copy of, like a hostage holding up the daily paper as proof of life. (You don't need to bring photos to a cartoon audition, but since this was my first one, I didn't know that yet.) The young crowd sat, our feet swinging from bucket seats, grim with anxiety but still gleaming with the odd professionalized sheen of the child actor. There was, as there always is at an audition, exactly one kid running lines out loud with their parent. This was, as it always is at an audition, a *Hunger Games*–style flex for that parent's benefit.

At that point, I'd only been on the audition circuit for a few months. I'd gone for a handful of on-camera casting calls and struck out every time, but I took it on the chin. My parents made sure I knew it was a numbers game and not simply a talent one; that, when you go out for a role, you're more likely to lose it than land it. At the same time, I was starting to wonder if my luck was spoiled by more than the usual odds. When I stepped in front of a camera and the casting team got a good look at me, it wasn't about numbers *or* talent, but something else entirely: I'd stand on the little taped *X*, emote like I was gunning for the Emmy, and hear as if on cue, "Could you do that a little more *street?*" Casting directors tossed off the phrase as casually as asking me to play it more natural or desperate or sexy. They never modeled or explained what they meant by it because, while that would have been helpful, it also would have been a human rights violation. But this feedback—if you can call it that—was a beat-cop sentiment buried in a polite liberal ask. It assumed I was fluent in white fantasies of how Black people *really are*, and that I was game to act out those fantasies for money. Though I didn't understand exactly what the casting teams were asking for, you don't have to grasp all the words to perceive the intent—their displeasure that my body was hawking goods my mouth didn't deliver. Eventually, I got used to hearing it—and ignoring it. Not out of resistance, but more like denial. If they weren't going to explain it, I wasn't about to agonize over how to do it. This also meant I got used to auditioning and never being called back.

Sitting at the *Berenstain* casting call, I hoped voice work would be different. For cartoon auditions, actors have to prepare a part of the script, which they'll read and record in studio in front of the creative team. I'd been sent pages from the first episode, a scene in which Sister Bear—the role I was reading for—delivers math homework to Brother Bear, who's been home with the flu. Sister spots a stack of blank worksheets next to Brother's bed, where they've lain untouched since she delivered them every other day that week. Rather than expressing sympathy, Sister Bear, who is very Type A, says something judgmental about how far behind he's fallen in class. (Brother, to be fair, is looking pretty vital as he lives his best life, smashing dinosaur toys together while *The Bear Stooges* blares from a

3

TV by his bed.) These bears live in a strict and unforgiving moral universe, where the sin of ignoring your homework is not mitigated by the trials of flu recovery. Later in the episode, Brother must pay.

A production assistant came to fetch me from the waiting room and walked me through a network of offices and editing suites. The halls were lined with posters of shows that had been produced there, an impressive history of the place that was also a partial history of my childhood. In the studio, it was dark and close. Nearly every surface was covered in felt or foam to dampen the sound quality. I could see the production team through a double-paned window, and they could see me, but I still felt invisible in a way that I liked. I remember not knowing what to do with my body, but also intuiting that that worry was pointless. After the eye of the camera, standing in front of the mic felt like getting away with something—a way to harness authority with none of the terror of visibility. Like impersonating your mother on the phone.

As with most people, I don't think I could have told you what my voice sounded like until I heard it played back to me. Apparently, when I opened my mouth, it gave way to some *Snow White* shit. Birds chirped and brooks babbled. It was the voice of a Type A bear, a voice that fit within a strict and unforgiving moral universe, a voice that chimed with the innocence newly in style. After a round or two of callback auditions, I booked the gig. Not long after, I left screen work behind altogether and surrendered, in joyful relief, to cartoons. That acoustic space of chirping birds and babbling brooks became my calling card—I've voiced a lot of squeaky, wide-eyed animals, and a generous serving of Strong Female Lead. Two decades later, I still work in the field, though I can only approach the purity of my sonic youth asymptotically. But every time I'm on the mic, I still thrill with the sense of invisibility like it's my first session.

I got into animation at an objectively good time, but that timing was also very personal. The idea of cartoons as a refuge from showbiz racism is part of my origin story. It also made certain facts easy to get invested in: that voice work was more about talent and less about looks or numbers. That reading for a wider array of characters meant I could more fairly prove my worth. While these things are true, if you believe in them too hard, you'll miss other truths that are equally valid. In cartoons, the offenses were less egregious than what I saw elsewhere, but they were still present, embedded not just in who gets cast, but who gets to write, direct, run the show, or get in the door at all. Naming the flaws in a world that's nurtured me is part of growing with and within it, of loving something vigorously and well. It can't all be the masochistic thrill of taking direction and the obliviating play of pretending I'm a bear.

Even then, I was still tripped up when animation's color-blind casting attracted public critique for casting white actors as racialized characters. For one thing, I didn't know that many people cared about us: drawing animated bodies has traditionally been seen as a lower art; so, too, at least compared to on-screen work, has voice acting. People joke that we can go to work in our pajamas (we don't do that; it would be unprofessional). Once, when I was fourteen and posing uneasily on a red carpet at a Hollywood awards ceremony for child performers, a photographer told me I was "pretty cute for a voice actor" *while he was taking my picture.* But my surprise at the criticism wasn't because our industry is free of issues, or because I had an idealism hangover. It was from how off the proposed fix seemed and how quickly it came into being. To solve industry inequality, production-side staffers announced, we must strive for perfect alignment between the body of the voice actor and that of the character. So we'd have the whole wide, rippling pool of Black talent competing for all two of the roles the creative team happened to design and script accordingly.

———

IN JUNE 2020, actor and comedian Jenny Slate posted a statement on Instagram sharing her decision to step back from voicing the character of Missy, a young Black girl, on the animated show *Big Mouth*. By that point, Slate had been in the role for three seasons and had wrapped on a fourth. She'd tamped down her early doubts about being cast by focusing on Missy's mother—who, like Slate, is a white Jewish woman—and on that basis felt it "permissible" to speak as the daughter, whose father is Black. But, by late June, Slate's feelings had taken a turn, as had the industry's sense of what *permissible* was. "Black characters on an animated show," Slate wrote (and the new rule went), "should be played by Black people." As I read this, my mind indexed back through every character I'd ever been called in to read for and I thought, not entirely disingenuously: What *Black characters?*

At the time, Slate's relinquishment of the gig looked sudden. But watch a few episodes of *Big Mouth*'s fourth season, and you can hear the racial anxiety simmering in real time, often played up for comic effect. *Big Mouth* follows a group of teens as they navigate the feelings and fluids of puberty—a practical hurdle for cartoons that employ real kids, as you often have to replace them as soon as their voices change; partly because of that consideration and partly because of how explicit it can be, *Big Mouth* is voiced by adults. By the fourth season, Missy's arc has evolved from first crushes and exploring her body to discovering herself as a Black woman. That latter journey is made rockier by her parents' post-racial attitudes and—in one of Missy's many winks to camera in Slate's later episodes—the baggage of being "voiced by a white actor who is thirty-seven years old." In an interview with *The Hollywood Reporter*, Andrew Goldberg, one of the show's co-creators, noted that that particular joke was written a year before Slate's departure—they wrestled with the appropriateness of her casting for a long time. The creative team, Goldberg explained, wanted to "acknowledge [her whiteness] in some way and not just pretend it didn't exist."

They acknowledge it a lot. The season's full of that type of in-joke, which feels faithful to the character's charming neuroses but also, in hindsight, like a way to buy time before something explodes. "N-word alert!" Missy brays when one of her two older cousins—who are played by Lena Waithe and Quinta Brunson—tosses out a "niggas ain't shit." We know Slate can't say it; Missy's inevitable, direct-to-camera admission of that fact falls a little flat. But, at other times, the way *Big Mouth*'s writers pluck at the tension produces moments of truly delicious comedy, ones that glean their very charge from the mismatch between the Black girl we see and the white one we hear. Returning from the salon where her cousins take her to get braids, Missy finds her mother less than enthused about her new hairstyle, musing over whether it's "manageable." In retaliation for the microaggression, Missy bellows, *"Stop stealing our men!"*—a line made exponentially funnier by the shock of hearing it appropriated by a nerdy white-girl tremolo. These writers are having fun. But there's a dark fascination, too, in knowing the chronology; that the team was spinning gags while treading water, trying to pack a Blacker character into the mouth of a woman incurably white. How much longer would it have gone on, if more people hadn't started paying attention?

Two months after Slate stepped down, and following an extensive search, the Missy gig went to comedian Ayo Edebiri, who'd previously been hired to join the *Big Mouth* writers' room. Hers was the most public recasting that followed the wave of white resignation, but it wasn't the last. Less than a day after Slate, Kristen Bell announced she would cease voicing Molly, a Black girl, on the animated musical show *Central Park*. Bell, a white woman, had published a bestselling children's book about difference and tolerance a few weeks prior—called *The World Needs More Purple People*—a detail that was conveniently kept out of this discourse. (Both Slate's and Bell's characters have one white parent, and a part of me now wonders if the creative teams were abruptly course-correcting from their belief that these daughters weren't *actually* Black.) It was also the end of Mike Henry's twenty-plus-year stint as *Family Guy*'s Cleveland Brown. *The Simpsons*, another show with a legacy of cross-racial casting, put out a blanket statement promising they "will no longer have white actors voice nonwhite characters." Something, it seemed, was changing.

But as I watched these desertions from inside the industry bubble, things felt more confusing than empowering. The cartoon community knows it's not exempt from the homogeneity that blanches every other artistic profession; a number of preexisting initiatives, like union committees and conference sessions, have been grappling with these questions for years. But the principle that seemed to be crystallizing—from a data set of white American sweethearts doing some timely privilege checks—felt like it was based on the wrong questions, ones that didn't really contemplate how race "works" in animation. There's no real precedent for trying to answer that query in a systematic way. The reporting of equity in cartoons—things like surveys and other demographic metrics—tends to focus on either the makeup of creative teams or the visible diversity of their output. The stages in between, like who gets to read for a broad array of roles or who gets cast as whom in animated productions, don't really get their own studies—those numbers get lumped in with broader data-gathering in the film and TV industries. Segmenting people's attention in this way—*look how many women are in the corner office, look how many of these cartoon children are drawn as brown, and now look at the breakdown of our profession overall*—can make things, at least in voice work, seem rosier than they really are.

"Animation accelerates toward inclusion," crows the press release for a 2019 report, "Increasing Inclusion in Animation," by the University of Southern California's Annenberg Inclusion Initiative—which clearly has a strong grasp of its key words. The study, which looks at the gender gap in production-side roles, notes an encouraging female presence in executive positions, while parity in directors' chairs is still wanting. But the data also clarifies that these gains have been made mostly for white women, and the release concludes, more modestly, that there remains "much more work to be done" before the industry can boast comparable stats for racialized women. Women in Animation, a globe-spanning nonprofit dedicated to advancing female progress in the field, has pledged to enact 50/50 gender parity across creative roles by 2025. Their mission statement makes no mention of which women might preemptively be shut out of the battle to redraw the pie chart, or if they're planning to hone their outreach to bring more than just cis white women into the fold.

Content analyses follow similar lines. In a 2018 demographic inspection of cartoon characters, the Children's Television Project—a research program at Tufts University—found that 5.6 percent of characters in their sample of 1,500 were Black. The figure lagged behind the U.S.'s estimated Black population (which was then 13.3 percent) and the report concluded that, while viewers were seeing more white female characters (up to almost 33 percent), racial and ethnic diversity still had "a ways to go." A more recent, more conservative sample of Canadian content, emerging from the Children's Media Lab at Ryerson University, explored twenty-seven shows that were either fully or co-produced up north and that aired from 2018–2019. Among its more critical findings, like the minimal representation of Indigenous people and the total absence of neurodiverse characters, the report champions near-perfect parity between white characters and those of color. But the value of this 51–49 balance depreciates when you consider roughly half of those twenty-seven shows had non-human protagonists. Rather than count "plant/object," "monster/creature," or "robot/machine" on one side or the other, they were omitted from the stats on race. But they make up half the sample size—can you still conclude that the country's content is 50 percent "diverse"? The sample size was *only twenty-seven shows*, which feels in-sufficient as the basis for any large-scale conclusions, and should tell you more about the itty-bitty capital behind Canadian cultural in-dustries than the virtues of its racial politics.

Content breakdowns only tell a partial story. They presume that if the product looks sufficiently multicultural—in this case, if the body of the character is not white—you can infer diversity's pres-ence elsewhere in the pipeline, like the actor who voiced them or the writer who scripted them. But representation in cartoons doesn't have to trickle down from somewhere else. It might live exclusively in the drawn figure, or it might never live in the figure at all. It might only live in the actor's body. Or—and here's where things can get both dicey and delightful—it might live in the vocal performance. The demographics of my resume are a mixed bag for this reason: In some cases, a character's Blackness was not communicated to me till after I was cast. At others, I've gone in and played them Black because I felt like it. Other times, I've only twigged years later that a character of mine was coded as Black at all—though that's because the entries in my ledger look like *dog, hamster, bear, giraffe,* and *sentient napkin.* Racialization in cartoons operates more like a shell game. I'm positive at least some of those "plants/objects" or "robots/machines" were coded as *something.*

In a classic *Vice* piece from 2017, writer Sarah Hagi describes her sense, "like a type of synaesthesia, but for race and cartoons," that various anthropomorphic creatures are really and truly Black, even if they're not explicitly drawn or even coded as such. Her epiphany starts with Bugs Bunny—whose creator famously drew on Black folk tales and bebop's nascent "cool" aesthetic—but spreads to include such icons as the Pink Panther, Arthur (half Black, by Hagi's analysis), SpongeBob (white passing), and—this one kills me, it's so perfect—Cookie Monster (West Indian). Hagi finds, among Black viewers, the same tendency to assign race to animated, nonhuman personas; an extra imaginative step that helps forge a connection with characters in the absence of actual Black protagonists (and, in her sample, actual Black voice actors). When Hagi floats this theory to her white colleagues, she's met with blank stares—the markers of Black expression have been so well-digested by the form, they're only recognizable to viewers trying to glimpse themselves within it. Hagi's white colleagues lose the shell game, but the Black viewers that she talks to get it.

Race in cartoons works pragmatically, subversively, and improvisationally. The relationship between the two variables is weird and fun and funny, but it's also the product of an industry that's mostly shut out minoritized creatives, especially from decision-making roles. We wouldn't be having the same conversations about what's *permissible*, in other words, if Black characters weren't the visible frontline of a field dominated by white people. With the calls for justice that swept across sectors, there was a new zeal for rooting out obvious sins. In that light, animation's casting habits suddenly looked like we'd missed the memo. That we'd spent too long believing in the fiction that drew me to voice work in the first place: cartoons are a scruffy garden in which racial discrimination could never bloom.

AS OFTEN HAPPENS, whenever a fresh injustice comes to light in the States, Canada looks around like, *oh shit, do we have one of those, too?* Five days after Jenny Slate's statement, which also happened to be my birthday, national media set the question in its crosshairs. The journalist's email landed in my inbox, forwarded quickly like something sizzling and unwanted. It had been sent to several Toronto-based voice actors like some sort of cursed chain letter (*Send this to five BIPOC or you'll die of being racist in seven days!*) asking us to be sources for a story on race and cartoons in Canada. It was disorienting to even see those three concepts in close proximity, like my exes had started comparing notes. The story wasn't meant to be a smear campaign, the email assured us; the parties in question were simply trying to center the right voices in what was becoming a sensitive conversation.

Incidentally, I'd already agreed to an interview—a friend of mine who was working on the segment had texted me earlier in the day to ask. But there's a difference between saying yes to a friend and stepping up to speak for your colleagues. When I saw the request pinging around my professional networks, a thing that many people clearly didn't want to touch, the role of Expert Source started looking more like Sacrificial Lamb. In the weeks since the protests began, I'd already been weighted down by requests to expiate the sins of other fields—the lot of many people dotting majority-white spaces that summer—which involved large amounts of unpaid labor. Here, I glimpsed a fresh hell: risking professional jeopardy. Sure, I could sand down hard truths into pablum, but it's notoriously easy to offend creative power brokers. What if I said something that got me blacklisted? There was no precedent for airing animation's dirty laundry, and now the person that took the fall for the entire field was going to be *me?* I mean, I loved the profession dearly, but was this a reasonable thing to do for love? It was also, remember, my birthday—I turned twenty-nine right after the start of the so-called reckoning; it turned into a hobbit birthday where I gave away the gift of, you guessed it, more free labor.

I still took the interview, but I went in prepared to skate away from any precipices. On the call, I tried to explain that the voice world is more or less built to work in a way that produces casting like Slate's and Bell's. Cartoons have long traded on the mismatch between the bodies of actor and character—to make risqué jokes, to get a certain celebrity involved (which is partly why Bell got the *Central Park* gig)—but also because your appearance matters less than it does in other media. It's not like auditioning for on-camera projects, where they film your face so they can watch it back after you've left. In cartoons, the creative team will see you in the booth, but it's only when playing your audition back later, and maybe sharing the tape with people who've never seen your face at all, that the final call gets made.

Your standard casting breakdown, which gives an overview of the show and the characters, will often contain boilerplate language like "all ethnicities welcome"—not because they're courting cross-racial controversy; more like the opposite. (If the breakdown said "whites only," the backlash would be very different.) In the demographic surveys of cartoon protagonists from the 2010s, the percentage of female characters tends to hover around 33 percent; girls of color make up only a tiny fraction of that third. The phrase "all ethnicities welcome" is a loophole; back in the aughts, if I'd been benched until somebody wrote a Black girl, I may never have made it into the game. What's more, I *liked* playing white girls. I knew even as a child that they, like bears and giraffes and sentient napkins, could sound like whatever I wanted them to. "You want to make some money here?" says Danny Glover's character to LaKeith Stanfield's in the much-quoted line from *Sorry to Bother You*. "Use your white voice." The joke of the film is that the white voice sounds like a dweeby corporate drone. The truth of it is that the white voice can sound like anything.

But "all ethnicities welcome," while practical and well-intentioned, also waits until the last moment to introduce the possibility of equity. If this kind of reasoning existed further up the chain, then we'd have more culturally specific storytelling to begin with. In the 2019 Annenberg report, though 17 percent of the previous year's top animated shows were created or developed by women, only a fraction of those creators—three women out of twenty-seven—were racialized. Though 20 percent of women were executive producers, the disparity here was even greater—six women of color to seventy-seven white women. Across the chart, spanning a half dozen years of the annual number of women of color in writers' rooms, the percentages are mostly a row of big fat zeros. These are the people whose creative decisions cascade down into script and studio. The issue, in other words, isn't who's getting cast as whom. It's that any diversity that does exist in casting is often a product of last-minute goodwill rather than long-term investment.

Unfortunately, none of this is really what people want to hear in a TV interview. It's not sexy, it's not sound-bite friendly, and perhaps most importantly, it's not cathartic. Catharsis, after all, means you're one step closer to absolution. Like white actresses diagnosing their privilege, it feels like the prelude to real correction, if not correction itself. I'd run into, and thwarted, this dynamic a few times since we crossed the race Rubicon. White interlocutors in various contexts would issue the same demand: anticipation of my fury, eagerness for vicarious release, and toxic neediness when I didn't deliver. Like being handed the microphone and told to rage-scream so *they* could feel better. Newly emboldened by the frankness of workplace and media dialogue, they kept pushing me to get mad so we could finally get even. By a certain point, I began to get off on withholding.

The unsexy, non-cathartic truth is this: In the absence of other actions, the emergent calls to redraw animation's color line could result in a business even less hospitable to racialized creatives on either side of the mic. In 2018, there were 3 percent of lead or co-lead roles for women of color in animated films. There's a lot riding on that *for*. In this brave new world of perfect actor-character alignment, is that percentage ever going to increase? Who's going to be controlling these characters' narratives, or writing their lines, or green-lighting the show? Is the pipeline going to choke their creativity before it even blooms, because they're exhausted from feeling tokenized and overlooked in their entry-level studio jobs?

The animation industry has long had a vested interest in controlling how Black people sound, a history that's unrolled with few Black people in the booth and even fewer, if any, Black creatives in the room. Even if the numbers are trending upward and we are seeing more Black faces in 2-D (leaving aside, for a moment, the question of who's voicing them), rarely do Black people have a say in deciding how those characters should speak or act, or the types of stories their voices and bodies will be used to tell. Merely relegating minoritized actors to compete over the tiny proportion of roles— roles that remain largely conceived, written, drawn, and directed by white people—is a gesture that ignores animation's deeper histories. Put another way: none of this is new. We're simply feeling the latest tremors of the tectonic shifts that blasted this world into existence in the first place.

ANIMATION'S BIRTH STORY tends to get recounted a few different ways. There's the version that venerates paternal genius, the gospel of many a nostalgic cartoon-history website—Tex Avery swiping Black cool and grafting it onto a sassy rabbit, Max and David Fleischer marrying *sexy* and *cartoons* in Betty Boop's body—and then there's the telling that focuses on, well, the labor. Early in the twentieth century, when animation was still a soundless medium, ethnic stereotype was a handy wellspring for illustrators churning the content mill. Racist and anti-Semitic caricatures made for quick gags: they were based on highly visual cues, easy to draw, and familiar— and funny—to a broad audience. The trend continued when studios began to employ European immigrants, who'd poke fun at one another's cultures in their work. It was all, at least nominally, in good fun. But even as they redrew the lines of the in-group, admitting ethnicities once excluded from whiteness and Americanness, this clique didn't include any Black people—because, as scholar Christopher P. Lehman writes in *The Colored Cartoon*, "throughout the first half of the twentieth century, no animation studio employed a black illustrator." With no one in the room to say otherwise, the caricatures of Black people tended to be especially vicious, "showing little of the playfulness associated with other ethnic cartoons."

On top of being vicious, they were everywhere. Black people may not have been holding the pens, but Black faces were all over the screen. Or rather, a very particular version of Black faces. The earliest drawn bodies, many of which were anthropomorphized animals, borrowed their physical traits and undisciplined energy from another popular entertainment medium: the minstrel stage. Blackface minstrelsy, in which (usually) white performers would darken their faces, dress up, and imitate enslaved Black people for laughs, was early animation's source material. The traces of minstrelsy are pronounced in initial designs of Mickey Mouse, with his jet-black body and white mouth (and, less subtly, the fact that early Disney shorts were literally accompanied by minstrel songs). Cartoons, in other words, have never been race-free, despite collective fantasies that things might have been otherwise; as Lauren Michele Jackson writes in *The New Yorker*, the genre is "built on the marble and mud of racial signification."

In *The Birth of an Industry*, cinema studies professor Nicholas Sammond proposes a more direct relationship between cartoons and minstrelsy; one not of influence but iteration. According to Sammond, animation is itself part of a long tradition of blackface in American entertainment, not just informed by minstrel shows but an actual "permutation of [them]." "Mickey Mouse isn't *like* a minstrel," Sammond writes, "he *is* a minstrel." Many of the form's hallmarks—white gloves, bug eyes, big mouths, clumsy feet, resistance to discipline— were exported to cartoons wholesale and persist in such Saturday-morning mainstays as Bugs Bunny and the Animaniacs (or, to take a more recent example, the ladybug Nick Kroll plays on *Big Mouth*, a character with a pale, black-bordered face and thick pink lips, who's peripheral to the action but will pop in to bookend a scene with commentary in exaggerated Black vernacular). Beyond their aesthetics, minstrelsy and cartoons also share an animating impulse—to serve and protect the boundaries of whiteness. In the time of slavery, writes Saidiya Hartman in *Scenes of Subjection*, blackface performances were a kind of psychological balm for anxious whites. They "restaged the seizure and possession of the black body for . . . use and enjoyment," a promise that whiteness was an unbreachable boundary. Blackface minstrelsy redrew the lines between *them* and *us* even as it scrambled them through performance—not unlike how early animators used blackface caricatures to excise their own angst about assimilation.

A common refrain in this history is that characters were drawn this way because the designs were cheap and efficient. The high-contrast figures of early cartoons like Felix the Cat and Bosko the Talk-Ink Kid, with sharp lines delineating their bulging white eyes and lips from their blacked-up bodies, meant that their images were easily and coarsely reproducible. This in turn was good for business: Illustrators could crank out work at an even faster rate, which gave studios an edge as the industry's labor model shifted toward industrialized production. In an absurd pileup of appropriations, the 1920s also saw various studios stealing character designs from one another, and then getting aggressively litigious about it. To reap the rewards, then, you didn't just have to be the most racist, but you had to be racist *fastest*. Powering the whole engine were the sights and sounds of Blackness, which moved the dial on the form but saw nothing of the profits.

The arrival of sound brought fresh possibilities for both storytelling and stereotyping. The task of matching mouth movements to dialogue was a lock that animators still needed time to unpick. Enter jazz, which offered a new shorthand to convey Blackness: producers would sync the movement of characters with the beats of the music. Using Black music led to some flashes of positive representation—at one point, cartoonists would go to jazz gigs, check out what artists like Louis Armstrong and Cab Calloway were cooking, and concoct stories and roles for them based on what they heard—but it also opened the door to more explicitly racist caricatures of Black *people* than in early days of anthropomorphic minstrels. With jazz came the city; with the city, the sins of urban living—like gambling and drinking and sex—which fed into stereotypical depictions of Black life. Less subtlety was still possible: the plantation and "darkest Africa" were also popular locales to set to a jazz score. These white fantasies reached peak indulgence in the Censored Eleven, a crop of Warner Brothers short films from the 1930s and '40s. These films rely so heavily on anti-Black caricature that, as their name implies, they've been withheld from official circulation. They're easy enough to find online, though, as is the rabid community of apologists who cry nostalgia and—unimaginatively—censorship.

In this context, absent a cameo by a household name like Armstrong, Black characters were voiced mostly by white talent. There were some working Black voice actors, but without the stepping-stool of prior fame, it was harder to find a foothold in the industry (a present-day hurdle that many Black voice actors still have to clear, especially to land a plum gig like the lead role in a Pixar film). But antebellum stereotypes like the mammy and the Sambo remained in heavy circulation—the old trifecta of caricature's humor, efficiency, and profitability still held firm—and an actor could find steady jobs by consenting to play them. This conditional acceptance could be cruel and undignified: Black characters were often scripted, Sammond writes, in the "long, slow, southern, and stupid cadence of the minstrel." Nor were the marquee jazzmen immune, either—their natural vocalizations would sometimes be replaced by a phonetic rendering of whatever the white writers thought scatting was, a mess of syllables impossible to pronounce and referred to, in at least one script, as "coon shouting." (*Could you do that a little more* street?)

Even under these circumstances, performers like Lillian Randolph managed to build successful careers—in her case, by playing domestics in southern Black dialect. She voiced the beleaguered housekeeper, Mammy Two Shoes, in *Tom and Jerry*—a show that later caught heat for a few episodes in which its titular cat and mouse wear blackface. The show was a cash cow for Hanna-Barbera and, presumably, also a lucrative gig for Randolph herself. Having carved out a niche that included a similar role on the radio show *Amos 'n' Andy*, Randolph was protective of her hard-won career and critical of the anti-stereotype activism—including by the NAACP—she perceived as a threat to it. Their advocacy techniques, as she saw it, were well intentioned but poorly executed; more about standing on principle than improving the material lives of working actors. Such groups fought to get rid of caricatured roles, Randolph said, but then wouldn't push for those roles to be replaced by anything else. Though removing roles like Mammy Two Shoes might tip the scales in favor of better representation, it also meant there'd be one less job than before. "I am very proud that I can portray a stereotyped role," Randolph proclaimed in a 1947 interview. "When you take that away from me, you take away my birthright." No doubt she also knew, intimately, the perils of seeming ungrateful in a field that's made it clear you're not really welcome in the first place.

Randolph, and other voice actors who were trying to get paid, were in a compromised position. Though Black voice actors have more wiggle room now than we did in the 1940s, the core of Randolph's concerns strike me as dizzyingly contemporary. Today's calls for character-actor alignment have similar side effects to yesterday's anti-stereotype activism: both are well-meaning efforts to eradicate a problem and position equity as their slightly foggy end goal. But neither fully thinks through the implications for the people it's trying to protect. Neither avoids the risk that the pie might end up smaller than it was in the first place.

In later, leaner years, a version of the thing that Randolph feared came to pass: Mammy Two Shoes was phased out of the show, with the character redrawn as a white woman, renamed *Mrs.* Two Shoes, slimmed down, and dubbed over by someone else. Though the viewer rarely saw her face in either iteration of the character—her head was almost always cropped out of the shot—she was, after her whitening, allowed a few personal photos of a husband and kids that would occasionally appear in the frame. This detail, and the character's broader transformation, were reflections of the 1950s' spike in white, middle-class family values, which saw the decline of racist tropes—and, consequently, Black characters—in cartoons at the precise moment their stock dropped.

WHETHER A BLACK role is voiced by someone who "matches" the character or not, the bigger problem is the ivory grip on what *Black* sounds like. We haven't moved past this difficulty, nor is it restricted to cartoons, or any particular minoritized group. The cruelty of caricature makes its home in any context. Weirdly, it's not always played for laughs, either. Such was the case a few years ago, when the quarterly outlet *Fireside Magazine* retracted an audio version of a published essay. The piece, by hip-hop scholar Dr. Regina Bradley, had been recorded by a white man who'd chosen to read it in southern Black dialect (or, at least, his interpretation of it). In a statement, *Fireside*'s then-editor claimed he hadn't listened to the audio before publishing; on Twitter, he said he didn't listen "closely." My guess is that he listened just as carefully as he needed to, and the voice he heard was exactly the one he was expecting.

Or, to take a more notorious and intentionally comic example, consider Hank Azaria's Apu. There's a damning story, in Hari Kondabolu's 2017 documentary *The Problem with Apu*, of how the voice came to be. During a table read, Azaria was given the bit part of a convenience store clerk of unscripted race and accent. (It's interesting, in this line of work, to track when "it wasn't in the script" comes up as a defense, and who benefits from it—Lillian Randolph tried it to prove the use of dialect was her own creative choice, but the NAACP wasn't buying it.) But Azaria opened his mouth, the white people roared, and a star was born. The origin of Apu tells a familiar tale of layered white theft; in a 2015 TV interview excerpted in the documentary, Azaria claimed the voice was one part nostalgia—when he first moved to LA, most of the 7-Eleven cashiers he saw were "Indian and Pakistani"—and one part homage to Peter Sellers's brownface routine in 1988's *The Party*. (When it comes to picking a performance to publicly associate your name with, this is a hell of a choice.) Azaria's impression moved through a succession of white rooms that heard the voice, snickered, and agreed that this was *definitely* a good idea. Eventually, in response to long-standing criticism that included the documentary, Azaria stepped down from voicing Apu in early 2020.

To Kondabolu, and the performers he interviews—a group that includes Hasan Minhaj, Aparna Nancherla, and Aziz Ansari—Apu's voice typifies the bind of the racialized actor, trying to play a game when the odds are stacked against you: "Is it better to be clowned, or clown yourself?" Actress Sakina Jaffrey, whose notable roles include White House chief of staff Linda Vazquez in *House of Cards* and Mindy's mom on *The Mindy Project*, coined the term *patanking* to describe the "broad Indian accent" South Asian actors get asked to do on camera or on the mic. The term *patank* is phonetic, mimicking the blunt consonants and pulled-back tongue that makes an "Indian accent" sound believable to a certain kind of listener. The word found wide circulation among South Asian actors in the nineties, who'd walk out of auditions and ask one another, with a knowing care I find incredibly moving, "Did you have to patank?"

The most telling moments of the documentary come in an interview with Dana Gould, a former writer and producer on *The Simpsons*. When asked why Apu sounds like that, Gould parrots the 1920s reason for why Black characters had swollen pink lips and spoke in mangled dialect: "There are accents that, by their nature, to white Americans—I can only speak from experience—sound funny. Period." You can hear his squirmy distaste for naming the category *white Americans*. Sitting across from Kondabolu and his questions, Gould is under pressure to disavow a key tenet of his work and its history: that caricature is objectively, universally funny. Belief in that notion has sustained a lot of "edgy" comedy. The notion sounds nobler, and lends more heft, than "funny to the people in the room because the system is skewed in their favor." Like the early animators, Gould and his team were also on punishing deadlines, cranking out regular twenty-two-minute episodes over twenty-five years. Under that kind of pressure, caricature is a godsend: it's cheap, funny, and efficient. Fallbacks like catchphrases—"Thank you, come again!"—require little work to get the laugh. Gould doesn't quite say the *pace* of the work is the reason Apu has become such an extended gag, but you can sense urgency in how he talks about the push for laughter: "The bottom line was always what's funnier," said Gould. "Our job was to write a comedy." I wish Kondabolu had pushed Gould harder on whether he thinks the comedy actually stems from the jankiness of the accent—the fact that Apu sounds like, as Kondabolu puts it, "a white guy doing an impression of a white guy making fun of my father"—or the more disturbing option, which is that the creative team thought Azaria's accent was accurate, and that anyone who sounds even vaguely like that is automatically funny.

In an essay for *The New Yorker* on Kondabolu's documentary, Hua Hsu places Apu in a longer lineage of racialized characters that seemed like a good idea at the time. Hsu cites Harriet Beecher Stowe's Uncle Tom and Earl Derr Biggers's Detective Charlie Chan as creations that "were invented to thwart stereotypes"—the respective causes being abolition and countering anti-Asian racism—"only to end up advancing different, softer, no less racist stereotypes in their stead." Granted, the degree of virtue is diluted in *The Simpsons;* Apu was already a stereotype to start with, developed by white people playing on clichés of the "good immigrant." But he's also genial, hardworking, and, in an earlier era, a fan favorite. "Good intentions sometimes lay bare a kind of chummy condescension," Hsu writes. The condescension goes deeper than just casting Hank Azaria. Even if the role had been voiced by a South Asian actor, there *still* would have been a problem with Apu. There's a difference between leaning into animation's capacity for play—whether it's benign or more subversive—and letting the white imagination dictate the terms by which any racialized voice can speak at all.

The elasticity of voice work clearly has its limits. But it's also true that "getting it wrong" on purpose can be magic. One of cartoons' chief virtues, after all, is that the sonic isn't always bound to the visual. I don't think I laughed harder while watching *Big Mouth* than when Missy brayed at her white mom to "stop stealing our men." In Aaron McGruder's *The Boondocks*, a pair of inept ex–special forces soldiers, Ed Wuncler III and Gin Rummy, are drawn as white but voiced by two Black men, the late Charlie Murphy and Samuel L. Jackson. Their casting sparks a jolt of recognition, or rather, *mis*recognition, in the listener—you know right away, as you're intended to know, that these are not "white voices." With Jackson especially, you're meant to recognize exactly whose voice you're hearing—in Gin Rummy's very first scene, his character recites some of Jackson's infamous *Pulp Fiction* dialogue. Casting Murphy and Jackson is a sharp, efficient piece of character work: when you hear these two trigger-happy white boys talking Black, you know right away what they value, what kind of media they consume, and who they like to think they are. It twists the ugly histories of animation and minstrelsy, drawing power from *getting it wrong* rather than having power snatched away by the same mechanic. It's also, after years of hearing so many Black voice actors "talk white" so that they'd get the job, deeply satisfying.

NOWADAYS, CASTING CALLS that land in my inbox can feel like they're trying very hard not to offend me. I've noticed, anecdotally, a small uptick in characters who are explicitly identified as Black; I sense, also anecdotally, that producers feel freer in saying it, and in seeking tapes from actors whose backgrounds align with it. Along with that inflated sense of permission, though, have come narrower parameters for how a character—whom everyone agrees is Black in every way—ought to sound. Sometimes, it isn't enough to cast a Black actor and let them find the role's sonic space. The project is committed to doing right by the communities it represents. The team wants children, who've spent so long grasping at the crumbs of racially coded sentient napkins, to stare at the screen and be catapulted into the mirror stage. In other words, they might want the actor to sound, you know, *Black.*

How do you ask for something like that without being racist? Words like *fierce* or *sassy* are often called upon as supposedly neutral descriptors. Some clues are working overtime to give off the hint, like a phrase of dialect nestled among the otherwise dull English sentences of the character description: *13–17 years old. This girl is a badass. She don't care.* Look: We get it. You don't have to do that; it embarrasses us both. A tactic even less helpful is when creative teams name-check vocal references, which almost always ends with lumping together Black celebrities who sound nothing alike. A character will be like Lizzo but also, somehow, Viola Davis? Chris Rock, but with a dash of Denzel? Do they realize that these people have entirely different voices and affects? As the asks become more specific, they raise a more worrying possibility: when you plug the same adjectives into the same machine over and over, you're only going to get so many different results. Across intellectual properties, I see Black feminine characters circling the same tired tropes—she's fierce, she takes no shit, she's unflappable, resilient, and so, so cool. Pulsing beneath these polite tricks of language is an anxious refrain: *This is what you wanted, right?* No. That is not what I meant at all. The delight of this job comes from seeing a script and a character sketch and pushing myself to craft an uncharted sonic space for them to live, like a zany kind of negative capability.

After more than two decades of doing voices, the demand that confuses me most when I see it in casting calls is to sound "natural." Not for any reasons related to racial caricature, but more that I've grown so acculturated to the language of the microphone—flattening my long-since-rounded Canadian vowels to appease American listeners, sharpening my plosives to avoid the dreaded pop of air, thinning or thickening my timbre to slip between different ages—that I'm no longer sure what it means to sound like myself. There's freedom in being able to vanish like that. It means I'm good at my job. But, more and more, I see fewer opportunities for that display of talent if you're a voice actor and Black. Creative teams have memorized the platitudes that "Black characters should be played by Black people" and "representation matters." With the best of intentions, they tune their frequencies to what they hear as "a Black voice" and set out to find it. The problem, though, is whose finger gets to be on the dial: The sound that can emerge is less a voice than an echo, a negative of the desire that calls it into being.

Behind this new vocabulary is another messy, coded concept—one that kept cropping up when the wave of white actors stepped down. "I am happy to relinquish this role to someone who can give a much more accurate portrayal," Kristen Bell wrote in her Instagram caption. "We look forward to being able to explore Missy's story with even greater authenticity in the years to come," *Big Mouth*'s co-creators said on behalf of the team. "[We will] give Molly a voice that resonates with all of the nuance and experiences of the character as we've drawn her," read the *Central Park* group statement. Each declaration makes a similar concession—the real sin wasn't one of appropriation but mimesis. Each statement also dangles a similar carrot—that to recast a Black actor will bring the product one degree closer to the real thing.

I don't doubt the truth of their desire to get it right, or at least to avoid the shame and expense of further censure. But if you're going to dangle a carrot, *authenticity* seems like the wrong choice. It's rarely been the point of animation, for one. But also, authenticity according to whom? Are the actors' voices the only place where such authenticity is going to live? (Decades of respectively answering *white people* and *yes* to these two questions is arguably why cartoons have such a fraught history.) Black life and art disproportionately attract the hunger that we'll perform the authentic, the real, the soulful, the street; the expression of some hard-won truth that bourgeois white life lusts for but can't touch. That jacks up the expectations when it comes to what we sound like. As Hannah Giorgis writes in *The Atlantic*, this kind of "vocal 'authenticity' [is] only ever demanded of black actors." The expectation weighs on us more heavily than on white performers; I sensed this when I closed the door on film and TV. But those same tendencies I thought I was escaping are seeping into voice work under the banner of equity. We're living through the dawn of a new authenticity boom.

In *The Birth of an Industry*, Nicholas Sammond connects the desire for authenticity to late 1960s liberal guilt. White people fantasized about consuming Black art and culture as a form of penitence; a way to redress the sins of their forefathers. But, more than gesturing at pseudo-reparations, it also offered an escape from white, middle-class existence, in which the chief sin was dullness. White life was boring, but Black life crackled. The Blackness they longed for, though, was always idealized, pared down to its essence—*soul* is the word Sammond uses. *Soul* is also the name of the first Black-led Pixar film, which starred Jamie Foxx as a jazz pianist who falls to his death in an open sewer, mere minutes into the film. On social media, some viewers criticized the film for only letting him exist as a Black man for a few scenes, before he crosses into the spirit realm and spends most of the picture as a colorless ghost voiced by Foxx or, after a messy spiritual shuffle, a visibly Black man voiced by Tina Fey. (Disney's *The Princess and the Frog* received similar criticism in 2009, when the company's much-lauded "first Black princess" spent most of the feature small, slimy, and green.) In press for *Soul*, the creative team—which was studded, but not helmed, by Black talent—spent a lot of ink and minutes talking about the myriad ways they'd devoted themselves to getting it right.

Until animation does invest in minoritized creative talent, which will be a long-term project, the majority of human roles will still be white. To hold out for a perfect score on phenotypic matches with the actors would shut too many of us out until further notice. These trends haven't turned into dogma, at least not yet—I still audition for characters I both do and don't look anything like—but the seg-ment of the pie is shrinking. If and when the industry does make those changes, and a higher proportion of minoritized creators fi-nally gets creative control, we shouldn't be holding out for a perfect score then, either. This is animation! When has "getting it right" ever been the point, and why would we impose that sanction now, just when we're teetering on the edge of a more inclusive field? The people who've been shut out of the field deserve the full, troubled tool kit to make their stories talk back. I want subversion. I want caricature. I want the unnerving surprise of the right voice purposely written into the wrong body. I want them to glory in every last twist of the knife.

Tiny White People

High school English didn't ask much of us. We were assigned two books a year, one of them a Shakespeare play and the other short, cynical, and twentieth century. Never anything later than the '50s, as if literature had expired along with Willy Loman in *Death of a Salesman*. We peered into stories like windows, not mirrors: Look at these people and their odd, brutal lives that are nothing like yours. But they were. When I looked up from the page and over at my peers, the slide clicked into place. We were public-school kids and not prep-school ones, but *The Catcher in the Rye* must have hit home for some of them, white and upper middle class and angry their lives had denied them some essential realness. Like Holden Caulfield, they got kicked out of school, albeit not for flunking math—their parents hired private tutors for that—but for smoking weed. Coming back from lunch period, I'd sometimes climb the front steps past flashing blue and red lights. This was 2008 and before weed was legal in Canada, but calling the cops was just a flex. The borders of our neighborhood, a suburb north of Toronto, were so well pruned—high net worth, low crime, always voted Conservative—that policing was often closer to theater. Kids mimicked this impulse to regulate and practiced it on the small visible minority. *Lord of the Flies* intuitively made sense to me. I had no doubt, if we all got dropped on an abandoned island with no oversight, whom the group would turn on first.

The course books were kept in a locked back room that I rarely saw teachers visit after the start of term when they handed out the assigned titles. No one ever asked why we read *these* books over others, least of all me. Texts didn't seem chosen so much as ordained, random acts of literature I trusted were part of a grander plan. The books often had creased covers and edges rubbed soft, but their insides were barely touched—only penciled with phrases, like *man vs. society* or *wheel of fortune imagery*, which corresponded with what we got tested on. Other books hadn't been handled at all. A teacher once gave me a copy of *The Joy Luck Club* for fun, and it had obviously never been opened. Amy Tan was my only evidence that some writers of color were kept inside the locked room—they just weren't let out to frolic with the depressive white people on the syllabus.

Not that I made this connection at the time—I loved depressive white people. I loved it all. I loved how bitchy J. Alfred Prufrock got about not wanting to go to a party, which is exactly how bitchy I get about not wanting to go to parties. The way Gregor Samsa kicked his sorry bug legs in the air. Hamlet's highly quotable jackassery. Tennyson's weepy little mustache poems. At seventeen, I was indiscriminate and flamed at any kindling. I wanted to be a highly quotable jackass. I was also attracted to discipline and was easily trusting, and I'm lucky *book list* was the soft place where those things converged. (Though even then, if you're a girl asking older male authority figures for book suggestions, you won't get away unscathed—you'll get *Lolita* and a hand on your leg.) If you told me to read it, I would; if you said it was great literature, I'd probably believe you; if you assigned me a five-paragraph essay on it, I'd write you ten for extra credit. But I was also starting to pick out the contours of what made books objectively good. This seemed a skill worth sticking with.

I'd been a middle school polymath but, by the time I got to high school, I understood this was a lie. Subjects began to sort themselves into two life paths: things I could miserably brute-force and places where I might feel capable and even excel. Though my parents weren't thrilled that the former were math and science, narrowing things down was a relief to me—it felt like becoming a person. The academic transition wasn't easy on all students: in freshman English, girls who ran rings around me in the science lab would agonize over what a thesis statement was and how to write one. (But they went on to become doctors, so they're doing fine.) Once, on a test, we had to close-read the lyrics of "A Day in the Life" by the Beatles. As stoners bumped fists, a white girl known for her love of PowerPoint stormed out of the class in tears. (LinkedIn tells me she's doing fine, too.) *Yes*, I thought. *This is for me.*

It felt so much like mine, I took it out of the classroom. I wanted to know what happened between the Shakespeare and Kafka years, or after 1949 when Willy Loman wrecked his car. But even more than that, I wanted to be a part of it. A yellow legal pad records my summer reading between 2008, when I finished eleventh grade, and 2013, when I graduated college. These syllabi show an obsessive but incoherent course of self-study, cobbled together from best-of-all-time lists, teacher recommendations, whatever caught my eye at the local big-box bookstore, and a bottomless hunger to know. The idea of a canon was almost erotic to me; a complete system of knowledge that existed for me to consume and be consumed by. This aligned with how I absorbed pop culture more generally—which is to say, like a pompous tool. I believed that albums should be listened to end to end with no skips; people on TV should walk-and-talk; and books should be read in unbroken sweeps of time during which your cell phone isn't visible in your periphery (the only item on the list I still endorse). I valued a certain stylized laboriousness in my art, a showy self-seriousness that implied in its making what it demanded in its consumption: a pure focus that means art is your life's only demand. Years later, I'd come to understand the relationship between such aesthetics and whiteness. But that was still a long way off.

I have a hard time extending generosity to my younger self. It's easy to look back, from an era drenched in the language of representation, and heckle myself like a horror-movie victim for not asking what seems like the obvious question: literally, *what is behind the locked door?* I'm fine with never having been a reader in whom the need to feel seen bloomed spontaneously, if it ever bloomed at all—if anything, it made me a better reader. But it also made me, at least at first, into a very specific type of writer. I doubled down on feeling *unseen* with surprising zeal. I didn't just turn literary whiteness into a fun summer reading project. I tried to turn it into an entire artistic practice.

WRITERS HAVE LONG had a language for how whiteness warps the imagination. James Baldwin used a vivid metaphor to describe the sensation: the "little white man" who hovers nearby and passes judgment on everything you write. I prefer this to the more polite contemporary euphemism, the "white gaze," which sounds like it has an off-switch and ignores the way it can get inside you. The "little white man," by contrast, sounds like he climbs up your back and breathes down your neck and farts in your ear. He demands that you explain yourself and your people according to specific scripts; cries foul when you describe what it's like to live in your body; when you turn a nice phrase, probably hisses something like "but you're so *articulate*."

Toni Morrison has cited the figure as something she and Baldwin used to talk about. In the 2019 documentary *Toni Morrison: The Pieces I Am*, she mentions "the little white man that sits on your shoulder and checks out everything you do or say." Elsewhere, he's burrowed deeper: in a 2015 conversation in the *Guardian*, Morrison describes the man as having tunneled "deep inside of all of us," like a universal case of tapeworm. Or, a nearly universal case: when asked if she'd managed to dislodge her own tiny freeloader, Morrison replied—unsurprisingly, if you've read her books—that she never really had one to begin with.

But little white people aren't just a hang-up or a parasite—they're an aesthetic, a master key, a pedagogy. One way to tell the story of literature might be to chart this figure's trek across the body, like a game of Pin the Tiny White Man on the Big White Man. For some writers, he'd live in their mouths like a bit (like Raymond Carver, or Gordon Lish and his acolytes); for others (Hemingway, Updike, parts of the Roth oeuvre), the little dude was in their pants. For Franzen, maybe somewhere odd and nontraditionally erogenous, like his nostril. In a 2015 essay in *Tin House*, "On Pandering," Claire Vaye Watkins cites Baldwin's tiny white man and admits to a version of her own. Watkins, a white woman, also has a white man living rent-free in her head, except hers seems less like a brainworm and more of a smokeshow. He's not little—he's *tall*. He's white-haired, a chain-smoker, and hails from New Mexico. Looking back on her past as a reader and friend and student and lover, Watkins realizes she's spent an astonishing amount of time and energy "watching boys do stuff"—be it sports, video games, or lauded acts of literary craftsmanship. This girlhood pastime became the DNA of her creative life. For years, she writes, she's been trying to emulate the bad boys of literature so that *they'll* finally notice *her*, claim her as one of their own, and acknowledge how well she, too, can do the stuff. The stakes of the issue are, admittedly, different for white women: Watkins spent her life watching boys do stuff so she could impress boys. Baldwin spent his "watching white people and outwitting them so that [he] might survive."

This basically sums up the MO of my suburban childhood: impress the boys and get out alive, a maxim at which I only half-succeeded, or maybe a quarter. From school and my fanatical supplements to it, I intuited something similar to what Watkins describes: the books agreed upon as "great" shared a certain grammar. If you wanted to join their ranks, you better pony up and learn the declensions. Through high school and into certain college courses, the way we generally talked about books—as things that sparkled with objective, dissectible beauty—thrilled me. It seemed to confirm something I'd always suspected but never had words for: that in literature there should never be a *good for you*, only *good*.

As a result, my desire to write fiction lay curled inside of me for most of my teenage years. What thrilled me as a reader jinxed me as a writer. I rejected the dogma of "write what you know" because what I knew didn't seem beautiful enough. Currents of racism, administered at random voltages, tucked inside a cozy suburban life where little else happened? Sure, that was a diary entry, maybe a mediocre treatment plan for radicalization, but definitely not the stuff of serious fiction. My friends were a sweet, scruffy group of art and drama nerds who spent most evenings and weekends migrating between local parks and somebody's basement. When I wasn't a part of their stoned, slow-moving mass, people would grab fistfuls of my hair and demand to know where I was really from, or whose mother my mother was. It was a morality tale without a moral. According to the rubric I'd developed from my summers of obsessive reading, my life was dead on the page before I even put it there. When I dared try, the scenes were so on the nose, so patently, odiously *good for you*, that I hot-flashed with shame. Part of this agony was because my taste far outran my talent. Nor had I lived very much, or thought critically about the keyhole through which life passes into art (at that point, if you asked me to describe it, I would have sketched you something closer to a garbage chute). But I also realized that when I cast off lived experience and instead drew on the tropes of what I read—white people and the particular ways in which they lived—the words on the page came to life, or something like it.

I felt like I'd plugged figures into a basic formula, then discovered it was capable of hacking a complex system. Dealing in these conventions offered an answer to every problem of structure or plot or characterization. I gave my protagonists money-scented names like Arthur and Quentin and Vida and Adelaide and felt at once that I knew them intimately. Their conflicts and motives came mostly ready to use: Toxic marital unhappiness. Alcohol problems. Status anxiety. The markers of money but never a mention of it. Ditto their day jobs. *I* may not have lived much yet, but these people were living it up. Writing scenes of drawing-room banter and pillow talk and drunken ennui felt like a passkey to worldliness, a way to look versed in things I'd never actually known, like intimacy, marriage, and affluence. It also felt like leveling up as an artist without having to do the dull work of moving through the world. This, I understood, was what all those summer syllabi had been preparing me for. This, I knew, was beauty.

NOT ALL BOOKS could avoid being called *good for you*. Men got off almost always; white women, slightly less. But something happened when other bodies got involved. When mainstream culture addressed books by Black writers, language and imagination dried up. People stopped talking about what it meant to be alive, or about beauty and pleasure. They talked about the books like they were high in fiber. Or they barely talked about the books beyond how important it was for us to talk about them and how good we were for doing it. This isn't specific to one period in my education, because large chunks of it, like all of high school, didn't contain any books by Black or racialized writers at all. But it was there in extracurricular tips from teachers who "thought I might like them"; or tucked into a cursory, rah-rah-Canada history lesson about the Underground Railroad; hell, it was in the copy on the backs of the books my mother nudged across the table as I rhapsodized about Don DeLillo or whomever I'd anointed my literary deity du jour: *Visceral. Raw. Multicultural.*

The practice of reading Black writers badly is an established North American tradition. In the nineteenth century, there was a major publishing boom in slave narratives. Books by writers like Harriet Jacobs and Frederick Douglass were big sellers even in their own time. The accounts offered personal stories explicitly framed as "representative" of all Black people, adding fuel to the case for abolition. But even with such high stakes, writers had to hold a lot back. Mainstream readers had no stomach for suffering, or for being called out as part of the problem. Narratives by Jacobs and others are instructive in tone, cut out most of the writers' interior lives, and remain discreetly silent on the most graphic horrors of enslavement. But what really gets me is how much they had to, well, pander.

These writers had to suck all the way up to their white reader. They showered him with praise, Toni Morrison writes in "The Site of Memory," "by assuming his nobility of heart and his high-mindedness. They tried to summon up his finer nature in order to encourage him to employ it." These writers had a sense of their audience keen enough to rival contemporary marketing meetings at conglomerate publishers. They knew how fragile their readers were, how swiftly they'd lose sympathy and throw the fight if they dared to tell the whole truth or even a big part of it. In order to get white people to listen at all, let alone help further the abolitionist cause, the author had to spill ample ink saying how great the reader was doing for even picking up the book. Despite all that care and the high sales numbers, some white critics still called these books "biased," "inflammatory," and even "improbable."

The needle has moved since then, though further on some days than others. Even now, as the white reading public reappraises canonized works for their depreciation ("*Lolita* is bad, actually") and Morrison has a Nobel Prize to her name, people still look to *The Bluest Eye* as a guide for unlearning racism rather than an aesthetic achievement. The recent surge of antiracist reading lists was yet another reminder that the work of Black artists gets read, as Morrison put it back in 2003, "as sociology, as tolerance, but not as a serious and rigorous art form." Books explicitly framed as guides to antiracism were corralled onto "syllabi" alongside texts whose only educational aspect was that they happened to be written by somebody Black. Not only does this imply racism can be read away, but it also suggests a sameness between a literal guide (like *How to Be an Antiracist*) and a literary novel; that both can and should be read under the sign of white self-improvement. Two hundred years later, readers still needed coddling.

Nobody sat me down and explained this to me when I was younger. But it was everywhere, like *write what you know*—you just have to inhale, and it's colonized your lungs. I didn't have a strong grasp of what *politics* even meant in high school, but I was convinced that whatever it was, I wasn't going to let it get anywhere near me or my work. As a teenager, I had a specific model in this pursuit: Vladimir Nabokov. Nabokov famously sneered at collectivity, morals, or group affiliation of any kind. He thought such things had no place in literature. "The larger the issue the less it interests me," he told the *New York Times Book Review* in 1971. I was obsessed with him and enchanted by his tenet that good writing, even about obscenity, was purely a matter of pleasure. I even ran a blog in his honor, which I sent to my mom, a few friends, and—boldly—my first-year lit prof, who was nice enough to actually look at it. *The Nabokov Project* (dot blogspot dot com, baby!) still lives online, its posts many thousands of words long and archived against a backdrop of ugly mint green. The entries swerve between ecstatic regurgitations of literary theory, the swagger of someone who's never been edited, and an octogenarian's first time logging on ("At long last, I have mastered the art of the HTML 'underline' tags!"). They also, more generally, try to puzzle through Nabokov's theory of writing to see how much of his coattails I could stuff in my fists. Reading it now, I'm struck by how much permission I needed—from a dead guy, nonetheless. If I wanted to write fiction so badly, you'd think I would have just sat down and done it.

Nabokov's strong opinions on art and life were attractive in the way they seemed to confirm what I wanted, so badly, to believe about quality. He believed fiction should construct its own universe, one that was unsullied by the outside world. "Mediocrity," he says in a 1967 interview, "thrives on 'ideas.'" Note how he made sure *ideas* was in scare quotes. In contrast, he says, encountering true literary talent on the page stimulates "the sudden erection of your small dorsal hairs." His viselike approach to authorship guaranteed total control over how one's work would be received, a gift I thought I could earn before I realized it wasn't my birthright. I wanted my hypothetical readers' minds unclouded, the better to feel that hair stand on end; if they were too in their heads, hung up on things like which causes or identities or antiracist tenets my fiction *represented*, how were they going to get it up?

MY EARLIEST SHORT stories were drafted for creative writing workshops. The first was about a dentist and a musician whose marriage was breaking apart because the concert-pianist wife was in lust with the ghost of Sergei Rachmaninoff. Another story, set closer to home, was about bored suburban drama students making home movies. (They were also pretty desperate for sex, albeit with each other rather than a Russian Romantic composer with huge hands.) Those stories never mentioned race, which wasn't a conscious omission, but it was a comprehensive one. In hindsight, my objective is transparent: write what you think great prose looks like, since joining the club means speaking the language. (I don't know where in the canon I divined "fucking Rachmaninoff's ghost," but it doesn't feel like that big of a stretch.)

Though I'd vowed to keep politics out of my work, I felt constrained by that decision sooner than I'd expected—only a few months into the undergrad workshop in which I'd written those other two pieces. It was foolish to think I could cut out politics at all, but I saw so many people, on the page and on the street, seem to live their lives free of it that I thought I could give it a shot. But trying to sidestep racial dynamics in my work meant closing off too much of the world and how I experienced it, which in turn choked what happened on the page. This felt unfair, but also true, which meant I had to listen to it. Agreeing to talk about race in my fiction felt like volunteering for that *other* category—good for you, high in fiber, rah-rah-Canada-Underground-Railroad. But there had to be a way to do it that avoided the trap. After all, white people don't just write about white people. I initially broached the subject in a story that reads like a bunch of cutting-room-floor scenes from *Guess Who's Coming to Dinner*. It's titled, should you miss the reference, "Guess Who's Coming to Dinner."

The story opens on a white couple, Laura and Greg, drifting down the freeway. They have serious communication problems they don't bother trying to hide from their children in the backseat. The family is on their way to meet some long-lost cousins they've only just learned about. When Laura's father died, she met one of them— a mild, blazer-wearing academic called David—at the funeral. Later, David reached out to set up a dinner. The only hitch? Laura and Greg get there and find out David's wife and kids are Black, which can be very traumatic for tiny white people if they aren't ready for it. The setup's very laborious, a criticism the story's self-aware about.

But the premise was actually lifted straight out of my life (though, thankfully, the characters were not). Rereading the story, I'm riveted by how awful Greg is. He's every cliché of toxic maleness: a bit of a lech who has no respect for his wife, thinks road lane markings don't apply to him, blasts sexualized Zeppelin songs in a car that contains his sleeping five-year-old. Worst of all, he's an *actor*. His literary forebears are clear; they're listed on a yellow legal pad that tracks my summer reading between eleventh grade and college. But Greg's also not the real villain here. He's just a foil for his wife, who spends the story convinced she's the victim of various small offenses before she starts downing vodka—at a pace that belies the fact I had no idea how to drink—and spewing some extremely racist shit.

In the story, Laura confronts the greatest hits of faux hot-button issues: Interracial love! Breastfeeding in public! Child literacy! While trying to prove how fine she is with all of it, she manages to utter every cliché about mixed-race family-making—mistaking the wife for the help; going gaga over how beautiful the kids are; comparing their skin to various caffeinated beverages. What I'm interested in, though, aren't the story's politics—those are as cookie-cutter as it gets—but its sympathies. It's weirdly gentle toward Greg, who exorcises most of his horribleness in the car on the way over. But the character who truly deserved better is Delilah (yes, she's really called that), David's wife and the plot's catalyst. In the story's circus of casual racism, Delilah is denied an inner life. Sure, she gets some of the most fist-pumping lines in response to Laura's indiscretions. But otherwise, she's flat, a bit of window dressing for the white characters to eyeball, tokenize, attack, and defend.

My solution, it turns out, was to pay lip service to politics. I dropped a Black character into the action to force a series of gaudy set pieces. Delilah was a lightning rod for everything I thought a white reader expected to see in my work—racism, Blackness, a sly knowingness about it all. Airing these things on the page, I figured, was a way to get the business over with so we could get down to pleasure. I could collect and control my readers' responses to racial dynamics, freeing up their minds to appreciate my fancy turns of phrase. I don't think it worked, but points for effort. Delilah deserved better, and the version of me that wrote her as an object was clearly working through a lot. The story, I should say, was handled with incredible sensitivity by the workshop. I was pretty lost at the time, and I'm grateful for their care.

This puppet-mastery was a way to protect myself, but it was also a form of imitation. In the works that I studied and the conversations I had about them, I'd only seen race talked about in a handful of ways, if at all. Race was a bit player, a walk-on, a punch line. A reality glimpsed by accident; a surprise guest at the dinner party. My literary models didn't have the vocabulary for meaningful encounters with difference. Difference, in the world of tiny whiteness, didn't exist.

IN 1992'S *PLAYING in the Dark*, Toni Morrison shines a light into the eyes and mouth of the U.S. literary canon and diagnoses what it's been avoiding: an honest discourse about race. Her beef isn't so much with the whiteness of the canon as much as it is with how scholars have talked about it—whitely, as if American literature were totally raceless. (She says, in a line that always thrills me, that her project stems "from delight, not disappointment," as if she isn't about to alter the field's topography.) Morrison is focused on a few major players of the nineteenth and twentieth centuries; ones, like Poe and Melville and Cather and Hemingway, who loom large as national literary daddies. What gets drooled over as "American" in their work, she argues, is actually a defensive pose, a reaction to living alongside Black people in the United States. The hobbyhorses of its writers, and the things that give critics the *Great American Novel* boner—freedom, masculinity, innocence, individualism—are responses to an "Africanist presence" onto which whiteness projects its fears.

American literature, Morrison argues, defines itself against this "dark and abiding presence" by calling innate the very things African and African American people were systematically denied. These anxieties might collect in the body of a Black character, as with Hemingway's *To Have and Have Not*, or it might be atmospheric, like the imagery of impenetrable whiteness that closes out Edgar Allan Poe's *The Narrative of Arthur Gordon Pym of Nantucket* (a vision of the South Pole so overwhelming, it kills off the one Black character). Put differently, Black people are a major reason why the canon is shaped the way it is. They're obsessed with us—though, as much as I'd love to read it, no white writer has had enough gumption, or perhaps self-awareness, to pen "Tiny Black People."

The project of much U.S. fiction is to do what the Constitution, Eurocentric education, and pop culture attempted before it: find ways to talk about race without really talking about it. What Morrison calls *Africanism*—all the flat, pernicious stereotypes Black people embody in the white imagination—offers white writers a coded language in which to both "say and not say," a way to simultaneously be "talking about" and "policing." In liberal circles, she admits, being elliptical about race is just good manners, and literary criticism has been a casualty. Good white liberals, like the books on the best-of-all-time lists, invite Africanism to dinner but would rather consign it to the sunken place than offer it a seat at the table. This avoidance didn't end with the twentieth century—it overflowed the historical bookend of Morrison's argument and evolved new tactics for the next era. Instead of simply being good *manners*, being squirrely about race became good *craft*.

For years, I kept a Gordon Lish quote taped above the desk in my childhood bedroom. Lish is a writer, editor, and teacher perhaps best known for his heavy-handed edits of Raymond Carver's work, which codified the latter's terse style. I'd first encountered this phrase, and Lish himself, in my copy of *MFA vs. NYC*, tucked into a harrowing set of student dispatches from Lish's former classrooms. The sentence, which I'd underlined heavily and transcribed onto a piece of card stock, was "Seduce the whole fucking world for all time." You've likely noticed, by now, that I tended to collect, magpie-style, the bits of culture that confirmed my preexisting opinions. This was another one: who wants to talk about politics when they're trying to get in the mood? In a workshop I took after completing my BA, I was assigned "The Sentence Is a Lonely Place," Gary Lutz's gloss on Lish's unpublished lectures. *Hell yeah fucking right it is*, I thought as I read it, *and absolutely nobody—my family, my background, my heritage—is allowed to live on that vast, lonely plain along with me.*

In *White Flights*, novelist and critic Jess Row explores the U.S. writing of the later twentieth century, starting with the big boys of the '70s and '80s—the literary inheritance that Row received as a creative-writing student in the late '90s. The lauded authors of those decades, like Dillard and DeLillo and Carver, probably aren't top of mind if you're making a list of U.S. writers who talk about race (though they *are* top of mind if you're trying to imitate how white people write). But in Row's readings, their studied disinterest in the subject speaks volumes. One of his chapters is on Gordon Lish and his perceived role in perpetuating this silence through his aggressive teaching. Lish pioneered and popularized a style that prized the sentence as a unit of pure voice and meaning. He aimed for "the deliberate exclusion of a certain kind of reference, observation, or sign," which often meant the details that signaled any particularity in the writer or their life, be it personal or familial or cultural or racial. The point of these erasures was to strip away the excess to find the essence of universal art beneath.

The violence of this erasure was both literal and figurative—you can look up images of Carver's stories after Lish was through with them; there's something forlorn about the few naked sentences peeking through the markup. Lish didn't have an especially light touch in class, either. According to students who took his workshop, he'd have writers read their work aloud sentence by sentence, each full stop functioning like a video game checkpoint that delays death for a few precious moments. When Lish heard a phrase that didn't measure up, he'd interrupt them (and destroy them). The problems with this approach are fairly obvious. For one, it's terrifying. If you can stomach the means, it'll get you results, but those results will also skew very similar—if you brandish a machete and yell at everyone to sound a certain way, they'll do it just to stay alive. If you take that machete to their prose, they don't even have a say in the matter. The method also involves a more symbolic violence. Compressing every phrase into Carver-esque minimalism translates every sentence into the same panicked Morse code of American life. Lish's pedagogy peels away the traces of perspective, style, history, identity, or—as Nabokov might have put it—*ideas* in the work, reducing anyone's prose to a thing that looks raceless. Whiteness gets reproduced through formal technique. By contrast, any writer who dares deviate from such a tradition—by, say, including material that's ethnically or culturally distinctive—is at risk of being dismissed from it.

Though Lish's style strains to express universality, it's not universal at all. As Matthew Salesses writes in *Craft in the Real World*, prizing writing that can't be traced back to a body doesn't mean the work has no politics, but that its politics are to seem apolitical. In a classroom built on this model, the minoritized writer is under considerable pressure. Short, tense, Carver-esque prose might not be her style, or the kind of work she wants to produce at all. But if it's an especially rigid workshop and she wants to be taken seriously, her best option might be mimicking the agreed-upon set of aesthetics to please the gatekeepers and barter entry. Of course, at one time, this was *exactly* what I was trying to do. I wanted to extract beauty from the mouths of history and politics like teeth. The idea of writing about myself, or my body, was horrifying.

In *Minor Feelings: An Asian American Reckoning*, Cathy Park Hong describes trying to anticipate, and outmaneuver, the expectation that her body would inform her writing. Arriving at Iowa for her MFA in poetry, she has already decided that "writing about [her] Asian identity was juvenile" and commits to formal mastery instead. She was right to be suspicious: in workshop, if one of her fellow students dares reveal a trace of autobiography, especially about race or gender, other students read it as a sign of weakness. This is the impossible bind of the minoritized writer: you're expected to write about yourself, but if and when you fulfill the prophecy, you'll be read as artless. Hong's search for "an honest way to write about race" follows her out of her MFA and into her writing and teaching career. In a season busy with public readings, she feels disaffected, "performing for a roomful of bored white people" for their approval. Later, when she's at home and watching the stand-up routines of Richard Pryor—who got his break writing jokes meant to appeal to a white audience—Hong wonders, along with Pryor: "What the fuck am I doing here? Who am I writing for?"

WHO WAS *I* writing for? Even at the time, I would never have said I was writing *for* white people. If anything, I wrote against them and against the sort of work I imagined they expected from me. I didn't go about it in the most original or sustainable way, but I was grappling with a weight that descended as soon as I opened up a blank document. Even as we reassess the canon and try to rebalance it, it's difficult to undo its more ingrained patterns—like the link between systemic disadvantage and the expectation that a writer represent it. The smaller your share of power, the more people your art may be mistaken as the mouthpiece for: Your gender, your culture, your

45

country. Some writers accept this burden as their political duty. Others find power in being a mouthpiece and it's not a mistake to read them that way. My favorite contemporary authors often trouble, or even reject, the calculus altogether. At seventeen, it seemed patently unfair to me. Even now, I'm still figuring out my relationship with it.

But maybe *for* and *against* are the wrong prepositions. Maybe it's more like I was writing *at* white people, or *through* them. The world I lived in and the ones I chased on the page vibrated in almost unbearable synchrony. I tried to harness power where I could. The white boys I sat with at parties, whose interest in me never made it past intense conversation as other makeshift couples around us peeled away for privacy, got transfigured on the page into the men who stared balefully out of windows and didn't fuck their wives and channeled their desire into vulgar fascinations with racialized women who didn't want to fuck them. The too-interested teachers became lurching man-children with big hands and terrifying appetites and weekly appointments with their analysts. The women in my life were almost always Lauras, well-meaning and overeducated and doomed to torpedo dinner parties with their liberal racism. They were my ways to imagine a world in which the stuff people got away with saying and doing and touching and taking had real consequences.

Of course, this is still a response to whiteness. If you're going to build a creative practice out of denying somebody's expectations, you still have to spend a lot of time anticipating their desires. But if you'd asked me then, I'd have said that I wrote for myself, and I would have believed that to be an honest answer. I wrote for myself, furiously and ecstatically, and then shoved those pieces in front of various people—my mother, my teachers, my peers in various writing workshops—and demanded that they find them funny and universal, the illegitimate heirs of the work of white American men. If a certain type of reader is only going to read my work like it's meant to teach them something, then I'm proud of my teenage self for feeling entitled to take the same liberty, reading the canon as if it were a guide to how a person on the page should be.

I haven't eradicated the little white man, not entirely. But I'm no longer tempted by his silky grammar, his weak tummy for politics. It wasn't a breakup so much as a gradual drifting apart. I finally started picking up the books my mother pushed across the table at me—turns out Zadie Smith is actually pretty good. I grew up, moved away, learned what my face looked like outside of the cubist refraction you get growing up around white kids. I read more beyond the books I was prescribed and cultivated a different goal: to capture what felt true. I'm grateful for my education in literature, the obsessive and self-imposed parts most of all. Literary whiteness has dug so many invisible tunnels through the collective psyche. But, my god, do I still love to slip into a book that's lousy with it.

I still have to flick away the tiny white man when he wanders too close, tries to climb into my ear. He watches more than he chatters these days, but he still speaks when spoken to. I avail myself of his knowledge when I need certain questions answered, like *would you call this color eggshell or ecru?* or *does what I've put on the page unsettle your dominance the way it should?*

Diversity Hire

W e need a diversity hire," announces Malory Archer in the cartoon that shares her surname. Malory is CEO of the fictional International Secret Intelligence Service (ISIS), a private spy agency that pretends to have government oversight. Her sudden social conscience isn't sparked by white guilt or a "racial reckoning," but money trouble: If she wants to keep up the long con that ISIS is a public organization—and therefore keep receiving federal funds—then she needs to sprinkle in a little more color. At the start of the episode, the only minoritized person on staff is Lana, a light-skinned Black woman. ("I'm one-sixty-fourth Cherokee," a white woman whines and is duly mocked for it.) This lack of diversity risks violating Title VI of the Civil Rights Act, which prohibits discrimination in programs that get federal financial assistance.

The office hasn't always looked this way. There were others, once; a string of racialized hires who all died mysteriously while working undercover. We see their deaths in quick flashback: each one, in succession, burned by an ill-timed drunk dial from Sterling Archer—Malory's son, and heir to a different type of positive discrimination. Malory doesn't know what happened to those men, or that her kid is to blame for it—just that the budget is in jeopardy. To rescue it, she hires Conway Stern, a dark-skinned Black man who wears a large Star of David chain and qualifies as a "diversity double whammy." When

Stern seems too good to be true, Sterling and Lana begin to suspect his vetting wasn't as thorough as it should have been. Theirs is a common reactionary response in affirmative-action cases, though their motives are less common: Lana is pissed by how quickly Stern outperforms her; Sterling, by how much his mom wants to climb Stern like a tree. It's a cynical universe, so of course their suspicions are borne out—Stern was planted to infiltrate ISIS—but in the process, the episode offers a sharp critique of corporate diversity initiatives.

As a concept, the "diversity hire" has a vexed relationship with equity. Warring within the term is a deep-rooted problem (*our workplace is too white*) and a quick, self-satisfied fix (*then let's bring in a single "diverse" person*). But the solution it proposes isn't a solution at all. It's been well documented that hiring a so-called diverse candidate, or several, is different from enshrining inclusion as part of a company's culture. Even if the candidate is good at their job—as Conway Stern is—the rationale for their employment may cast their skills into doubt. This is the point on which the *Archer* episode offers its subtlest critique of workplace whiteness. It has nothing to do with Stern at all, but the string of spies who preceded him and died in the field—Agent Ruíz, Agent Pak, and Agent Mgumbe. When Malory cites their names in a meeting, Sterling cuts her off by yelling "Loose cannons!" These men were sent on dangerous missions, killed by the lazy mistakes of a nepotistic white hire, and are now remembered for their incompetence. Sterling made the same pointless fuck-up three times, still has his job, and spends meetings yelling over his boss who is also his mom.

The workplace sitcom loves the diversity-hire trope. It's part of the form's relatability: just like our lives, the bosses are horrible, the tasks are tedious, and there's an alienated person of color in a majority-white office (a clear sign of whom the form is trying to be *relatable* to). This worker, who is often Black, is meant to remind the viewer, lest they forget, that there's still meant to be something squirmy-feeling about affirmative action. The same gag crops up across classics of the genre: *The Office* had its "Diversity Day" episode, playing the white dread of DEI workshops for laughs (with Stanley, Dunder Mifflin's long-suffering Black staffer, as the punch line). *30 Rock* keeps the joke on retainer with James "Toofer" Spurlock, a "double whammy" in the Conway Stern tradition, except instead of being Jewish he went to Harvard. Four seasons in, he learns, rather traumatically, that he was an affirmative-action hire. Enraged, he quits. These are the stories we tell ourselves about what equity looks like.

Nowadays, the term *diversity hire* carries more than a hint of the pejorative. Even if it's what a recruiter seeks, they know not to put that phrase in the job description. The principle of diverse hiring is sound and necessary—institutions should be made up of people that represent, even roughly, the demographics of society—but it speaks to a persistent systemic failure that we don't just call that *hiring*. Across sectors and institutions, notably higher education, the failure to turn equity into policy has been a famously messy battle. Courts, researchers, and corporations have floated so many arguments for why it's finally time: Diversity is good for the bottom line. Diversity is necessary to avoid getting sued. Diversity is just *fair*. At this point, we seem to have reached a broad acknowledgment that it's self-evidently just. But the principle of affirmative action is still under attack. The notions of meritocracy and competition are still defended like a crumbling fortress, often by the people who were born inside that fortress to begin with. And the on-the-ground labor of improving individual offices—what I'll call "diversity work"—still falls heavily on the minoritized people who happen to have gotten in the door. "Diversity hire" isn't the only phrase that's been discreetly removed from the job description. There's a whole slate of other expectations that don't appear in it, either.

———

FROM EARLY ADOLESCENCE I'd been tapped to sit on panels, usually to speak with and in front of other actors, about what it was like to work in the arts as a person of color; what it was like to be the diversity hire; what it was like, perhaps, to read for the sole racialized character in an office sitcom. For years, these events were the only channel through which I accessed the discourse of equity. Because I was so young, the form left its imprint on the content.

I understood talk of diversity as a kind of stress ball, an intermittent clench and release. The subject was tied to sensations that were intense but discrete: the expectation that I'd share my pain in front of an audience, or that I had pain to share in the first place, or that I experienced regular slights (like "can you do it more *street?*") as pain at all, rather than just annoyance. Then there'd be a Q & A. The session might be awkward, but at least it was over quickly. This, regrettably, became my schema for diversity work: conscription with no right of refusal, a sense that my presence was always at risk of being exchanged for usefulness, and the extent of my usefulness lay in agreeing that something was rotten. I understand, and even appreciate, the impulse to give a child a platform to air these feelings. I felt the frustrations of working in a field suffused with whiteness, even if I didn't have the language to express it. But without additional context—*here is what you have the right to ask for on the job; here is a committee who will help put these things into action; here is what you don't have to share if you don't want to; here is why we don't expect you, an eleven-year-old child, to have all the answers*—the panels made diversity feel like "that thing you have to get up on a stage and do sometimes."

I've been trying to offset this early cynicism without overcorrecting ever since. I find it hard to balance volunteer firefighting with the urge to watch the world burn—especially when I enter a professional or creative space with a bad track record for equity. Putting out fires isn't my job; acting like it is will mean that I'll burn out, too. But pretending I have no duty to act is unconscionable. I can't enter various professional settings and have the mark I leave be that I was "the only one."

As the efforts to topple structural barriers and increase workplace diversity have grown louder, diversity work looks different, too. Now, sitting on a panel to ritually air your grievances isn't enough by itself. Conscription entails a longer list of duties. Management may expect that you'll also fix the place up, polish it a little, patch the gaping holes. Again, I consider getting someone else in the room with me to be part of any job. But making that priority clear can often mean a whole pile of other problems get dumped on you, too. Employee satisfaction or retention, the ineradicable fleas of casual racism, snafus of public-facing language—these things absolutely need to be dealt with. But it's disheartening to step forward, express an honest desire to make a place better, and be told to rinse scum from dark corners management obviously hasn't thought to touch in years.

What makes cleaning house even harder is that the language of diversity has grown inflated. Cheapened by bad-faith histories and contemporary overuse, words like *diversity* and *inclusion* have entered the chat to block certain actions as much as to make things happen. In the late 1970s, the U.S. Supreme Court used *diversity* to make palatable what seemed radical—affirmative action in college and university admissions—and it has retained that placating trace ever since. Does *diversity*, with the starry-eyed naivete the word has come to connote, even express the goal of equity anymore? Isn't the catchall *BIPOC* kind of choked and gross? *Antiracism*, too, has had a hell of a watering-down these past few years. These words are so easy to circulate, it's hard to make real meaning stick to them. How do you achieve positive change if the language describing it has also been used, in some cases deliberately, to stop that same change from occurring?

———

IF IT'S HARD to express something true in language that's been emptied of value, the flip side is that it's easier than ever to say something while meaning nothing. This is part of why it was so easy to call bullshit on corporate diversity statements when businesses who'd never said boo about equity or justice started capitalizing on that ease. Even as corporations promised to do better, their action—or inaction—was the real barometer. Mark Zuckerberg announced a ten-million-dollar donation to "groups working on racial justice" even as he decided—despite employee walkouts—not to remove Trump's Facebook post that patently incited violence.

Noted Karen den Starbucks threw $1 million at a similarly hazy cause and vowed they would "continue to confront bias and racism"; less than a week later, BuzzFeed reported that the company forbade its staff—or its *partners*, since employees own stock—from wearing Black Lives Matter paraphernalia, or any "buttons or pins that advocate a political, personal, or religious issue." Customers, they suggested, might think baristas were trying to "amplify divisiveness." Hypocrisy was also evident in declarations by white-collar spaces like legacy media. Outlets that made centrism their brand craned their necks trying to find the content they'd long rejected for being too leftist; ostensibly feminist outlets saw Black and racialized workers come forward with accounts that gave the lie to the organization's public-facing politics; white editors stepped down from their jobs, ceding space at the very moment the glass ceiling shattered, raining down shards onto the fresh diversity hires. Even the company who sells Gushers, the gummy candy with the viscous liquid center, had something to say. Notably, they didn't upsell their intentions: "It's important that our words match our actions. More to come." Yes. But also: *Gushers*? Even at the time, many people felt that this was empty and bizarre. It's the "How do you do, fellow kids?" moment writ large, spanning all of capitalism. Corporations were saying these things because, at that moment, these things were especially easy to say. There was more to be lost by *not* speaking up. I feel a bland ease in cherry-picking these examples and a numbness to scrolling through the list, a litany of lost souls who all want the D.

In *On Being Included*, critical theorist Sara Ahmed's study of diversity work in higher education, she asks whether this kind of vow "commit[s]" an organization to doing anything at all. Antiracist statements are not, for example, legally binding. What we expect of them depends on how we read them: "If the statement is read as bringing about what it names," Ahmed writes, "then it could participate in the idea of [the institution] as being antiracist." In this too-charitable reading, the gulf between speech and action collapses altogether. It suggests *antiracism* is akin to folklore's Candyman: just saying the word calls something into being. But, as we've seen from the behavior of various companies, you can hit send on a statement and then turn around and violate it for profit. The written commitments often end up doing nothing at all. This skepticism, Ahmed says, is the right way to read such statements from the start. This part of her argument feels intuitive. The next part may not.

Building on J. L. Austin's and Judith Butler's work on the speech act, Ahmed suggests that a statement of commitment is *nonperformative* language that names a thing (antiracism, the proverbial *work*, etc.) precisely so the speaker can avoid having to do it. It's like *I'll call you* or *let's do lunch* or *the check is in the mail*. "[The] failure of the speech act to do what it says is not a failure of intent or even circumstance," Ahmed writes, "*but is actually what the speech act is doing.*" The antiracist statement makes nothing happen. It just creates the illusion of confession and looks like the first step toward recovery. Ahmed's definition of the nonperformative is an elegant extension of how we do, or don't do, things with words. But it also bumps uncomfortably against the more colloquial use of *performative*; the one that usually prefaces *allyship* and which people also use to name a too-convenient political insincerity. A business that nominally affirms Black lives while tamping down the same message is performative in the casual sense—doing it for clout rather than solidarity—because it's hypocritical. But this same hypocrisy also makes the statement *nonperformative*, because the company never really intended to help advance the cause. This may seem like semantics—and it kind of is—but a lot of people have fought about those semantics on Twitter. Both terms are trying to name a falsehood; both are trying to function as tools of accountability. But *performative* as Ahmed uses it—and its broader theoretical legacy—means the speech act has had some material effect in the real world. Not so for "performative allyship," which describes an empty gesture. I sympathize with people's frustrations over this theoretical quibble. White supremacy is too often invisible. There are few enough terms with which to pin it down without being told another one is off the table.

Whether we're fighting over what *performative* means or cringing at how the term *diversity* seems inadequate and candy-ass, we're dealing with the same kind of fallout. The discourse of equity has been used by lawmakers, CEOs, marketing firms, and administrators for the express purpose of holding on to power while pretending to look progressive. A lot of our present difficulty, in other words, is by design.

UNTIL THE 1970s, affirmative action's chief purpose had been to seek redress for historical violence. This motive sparked complaints on both sides of the partisan aisle about whether white people ought to be charged opportunity costs for their fathers' sins. But a 1978 Supreme Court case, *University of California Regents v. Bakke*, introduced a less threatening idea: that fraternizing with people from other backgrounds wasn't about making society more just, or compensating for past atrocities. Nor was it even really, or only, about race. It was about bettering oneself through exposure to different types of people.

In 1973, Allan Bakke received his second rejection from the

University of California Davis medical school. A blond, blue-eyed former Marine who couldn't quite call himself six feet tall, Bakke had fallen short of the minimum admissions score two years running. A recent national spike in medical school applicants made the process more competitive; in response to the demand, Davis had recently doubled its class size from forty-eight to one hundred. Applicants were assessed via two streams. The general pool competed for eighty-four seats and were ranked by grades, test scores, and interviews. If a candidate didn't meet the minimum 2.5 GPA cutoff, they were rejected out of hand. The same stats applied to the remaining sixteen seats, but these were reserved for people who identified as "economically and/or educationally disadvantaged" minorities. Applications sent to this stream were ranked separately and excused from the cutoff. Davis's med school had only been open for five years, but the administration was already trying to offset the embarrassing whiteness of the student body. Recent civil rights legislation meant that homogeneity was kind of a bad look.

At that time, the main rationale for affirmative action was still to remedy past injustices with present opportunity, a line of reasoning that made white people like Allan Bakke twitchy. Of course, Black people in the country had been deeply wronged—but not by *him*. He seethed as nonwhite students sailed into Davis, admitted through the special program and with lower marks than his. Moreover, Bakke was running out of time. His engineering degree, naval duty, and job at NASA had added up: by the time he applied to Davis he was already thirty-three. The program and training would put him near forty by the time he could practice, making him what most med schools then would have considered a bad investment. Though litigation is not the ideal forum for people short on time, Bakke decided to sue for reverse discrimination—albeit not for ageism.

His lawyer argued that the special-admissions stream was an unconstitutional racial quota forbidden by the Civil Rights Act and the

Fourteenth Amendment. The case wound its way up to the Supreme Court, trailing judicial and public opinions that either condemned or preemptively mourned the fate of affirmative action. People knew this would be a big one. The Court heard the case in 1977; all that time, Bakke was getting older, with fewer juiceable years left in him. On June 28, 1978, Justice Lewis Powell, a moderate Republican, gave the Court's decision: race could be *one* factor in admissions decisions, but it couldn't be enforced by quota. In Powell's eyes, this was an attempt at compromise. Though Powell wrote the judgment, the Court had split 5–4, and a handful of other judicial opinions partially concurred and dissented. The slim margin set the pattern for later affirmative action cases, most of which are basically variants of this one—a white student, rejected from an academic program, sues the school for reverse racism, and the Court wobbles without (yet) falling down.

The modern usage of *diversity* stems from Powell's opinion. A diverse student body, he writes, is a principle of academic freedom, a right that empowers universities to determine the who, what, and how of teaching, including who gets admitted to study. Variety is part of that bundle of freedoms: the quality of education, Powell writes, is "widely believed to be promoted by a diverse student body." Diversity is therefore within a school's purview to seek. But, he goes on, ethnic diversity alone doesn't clear the bar of being a "compelling state interest." (This is the standard to beat in constitutional cases, which receive the highest degree of judicial scrutiny.) The type of diversity that does pass muster—what Powell calls, a bit smugly, *genuine diversity*—involves "a far broader array of qualifications and characteristics," like being born on a farm or knowing how to talk to poor people (these are real examples from the decision). If colleges only look at race and ethnicity, they'd actually be working against the *real* diversity Powell's arguing for. He quotes approvingly from Harvard College's admissions policy: "A farm boy from Idaho can bring something to Harvard College that a Bostonian cannot offer. Similarly, a black student can usually bring something that a white person cannot offer." *Usually*. There are good versions of this concept, of course, like reminders for institutions to seek out and include people of many genders, abilities, neurotypes, etc. But there's also a common, bad-faith insistence that all kinds matter, like media's infatuation with the "diversity of ideas" (still a masthead of centrist white people, just peppered with a few more reactionaries) or attacking an all-minoritized lineup for its absence of white male voices.

The opinion is a logical extension of Powell's long-term agenda. Before his appointment to the Supreme Court, he'd been a director for Philip Morris, the tobacco company. Partly in response to scientific critiques of Big Tobacco, but also just out of conservative paranoia, Powell wrote a 1971 memo, "Attack on American Free Enterprise System," and submitted it to a private conservative lobbying group. Known as the Powell Memorandum, the document called for the aggressive protection of corporate interests against the radical left. College campuses, news media, and the arts and sciences were advancing a "broad attack." (The faculty who espoused such "Marxist" ideals, Powell added in a surprising aside, were also "often personally attractive and magnetic.") Not only were corporations taking a financial hit, but they were so threatened as to be a persecuted minority: "few elements of American society today have as little influence in government as the American businessman, the corporation, or even the millions of corporate stockholders," reads the memo, like a dispatch from a deluded universe. Later, after Nixon had appointed him to the Supreme Court, Powell would continue to push this thesis. He wrote a number of decisions that cemented the idea of corporate personhood—in law, the principle that businesses are people, too, and they deserve rights just as human beings do. Like farm boys from Idaho, corporations could also be hated and discriminated against (not just protested and demonstrated against). This is part of the legacy of *diversity*.

The Court reversed the lower judgment that race could never be a factor in admissions, but affirmed that Davis's special program violated the Fourteenth Amendment and mandated Bakke's admission to the medical school, from which he graduated and became an anesthesiologist by about fifty. People make uneasy jokes about the hidden bodies of their physicians' transcripts, but truly: Can you imagine finding out that the guy about to put you under needed a *court order* to get into med school? (This did not bother Justice Powell, who later became one of his patients and survived.) "There is a measure of inequity in forcing innocent persons in [Bakke's] position to bear the burdens of redressing grievances not of their making," Powell wrote in his judgment. In other words, Alan Bakke's personal hurt had turned into the law of the land: Of course, Black people in the country had been deeply wronged—but not by *him*.

FIVE DECADES LATER, these questions are still live. For anti–affirmative action groups, the Court's shaky stance is effectively an invitation to keep swinging. The latest try, *Students for Fair Admissions v. Harvard*, which alleges discrimination against Asian American applicants, may reach a Trump-tainted Supreme Court in 2022. At the time of writing, the Court has yet to decide whether or not it will hear the case. But, based on its present makeup, writes Nicholas Lemann in *The New Yorker*, "It's distinctly possible that the Supreme Court . . . could signal that it considers efforts aimed explicitly at helping Black people to be unconstitutional." This would be a devastating way to cap off nearly two years of a supposed racial awakening.

The tricky thing about compensatory justice, writes legal scholar Randall Kennedy, is that it "always entails an assumption or a finding of culpability." In order for somebody to make a claim in the first place, somebody else must have done something wrong. Looking at large-scale historical wrongs, that "somebody else" is usually white. But being held responsible can seem like its own kind of injustice. The diversity rationale, though, puts everyone on equal footing and doesn't point any fingers. By its logic, white people haven't done anything wrong, and they have as much, if not more, to gain from cultural exposure as anyone else. *Bakke*'s definition of diversity was the great equalizer. Ask not what you can do for systemically disadvantaged groups, but what those disadvantaged groups can do for you.

Canada, for its part, shelters affirmative action under section 15 of the Canadian Charter of Rights and Freedoms, which "does not preclude any law, program or activity that has as its object the amelioration of conditions of disadvantaged individuals or groups." So reparations are still, technically, on the books. But the diversity rationale has scrambled the signal here, too. If anything, when compared to the United States, the word probably holds even more influence as a national branding exercise. Despite more than a hundred and fifty years of evidence to the contrary, like the genocide against Indigenous peoples and a policing system that runs on anti-Black and anti-Indigenous violence, Justin Trudeau keeps invoking, as a chirpy national slogan, "Diversity is our strength."

Powell's *Bakke* ruling lit a fire under schools and businesses, giving them what Randall Kennedy calls "a strong incentive to engage in diversity talk." Regardless of actual commitments to inclusion, institutions learned to parrot the language of diversity—especially how *useful* it was—so that they wouldn't get sued. This didn't totally work, because a certain kind of white person can spot reverse racism no matter what. In 2003, two white women sued the University of Michigan—one of them for its undergraduate admissions policy, the other for the law school's—alleging that they'd been as badly treated as Allan Bakke. By then, the diversity rationale had ballooned so much, Michigan could argue diversity *itself* was a compelling state interest. Though the suits were separate, the Supreme Court heard and decided them together. The undergraduate policy, the subject of *Gratz v. Bollinger*, failed the test—their system, which assigned automatic points to all "underrepresented minority" applicants, looked too much like a quota. Almost every person who applied through that stream successfully got in. But the Court looked more favorably on the law school case, *Grutter v. Bollinger*, since the assessments were closely tailored to individual applicants. This seemed, to the Court, the right way to apply the rationale.

The real winner of both *Gratz* and *Grutter*, though, was capitalism. Commentary on the cases notes the number of amicus briefs—contributions from parties who are interested in the case's outcome, but not formally a part of it—filed by businesses that had been stalking the suit like vultures. The list included heavies like General Motors, Exxon Mobil, the American Federation of Labor and Congress of Industrial Organizations (the largest group of labor unions in the United States), and, most famously, the military. The Court, apparently charmed by this, cited the pile of briefs in their decision: "Major American businesses have made clear that the skills needed in today's increasingly global marketplace can only be developed through exposure to widely diverse people." In other words, diversity was no longer about facilitating cultural exchange for a good education, but about building a more efficient workforce—which is why so many titans of industry were suddenly invested in the outcome. They wanted universities to produce the best candidates for the companies to succeed. Powell's long game was still paying dividends: the world was a corporation and diversity was good for business.

The corporate world has continued to tout diversity as a tool of operational excellence. A 2015 McKinsey report, "Diversity Matters," charted "the relationship between leadership diversity and financial performance," defining diversity as a greater number of women and racial or ethnic minorities. The report concluded that the correlation was "statistically significant": companies with more varied leadership teams were likelier to make more money than their industry median. Such companies can also boast happier customers, more satisfied employees, better recruitment, and stronger decision-making. This is diversity in name only; a logical endpoint of privileging product over people. The McKinsey findings are specific to leadership—it's McKinsey, so they only seem to care about the 1 percent—but this top-down approach exemplifies another way justice gets coopted for the bottom line: by only letting in the "diverse candidates" deemed safe.

In *The Enigma of Diversity*, Ellen Berrey uses the term *selective inclusion* to describe how the women and racialized people who usually gain access to workplaces are perceived to be unthreatening by white decision-makers: they're of a high status, upwardly mobile, and expected to conform. If they kick up a fuss—about the whiteness of the company, say—then they won't be let in. Sara Ahmed calls such practices *conditional hospitality*, in which racialized people are only accepted if they "return that hospitality by integrating into [organizational] culture, or by 'being' diverse, and allowing institutions to celebrate their diversity." In that context, naming whiteness—often, naming power or politics of any kind—can become a problem. The presence of Black and brown faces in the boardroom bolsters a narrative of justice: sure, a thing called systemic racism exists *out there*, but not within the corporation. Also, everybody's getting richer, so stop complaining.

THE FIRST TIME I considered how workplace diversity would affect my life, I was getting ready to interview for summer jobs in law school. A year into the program, my peers had already taught me enough about farm boys and conservatives that I didn't want for exposure, though the farm boys hailed from Saskatchewan rather than Idaho. But capitalism was very much on my mind—the six-figure sticker price on the degree; the amount I'd spent so far; the ballooning total I still owed; and what summer funds I might build up to dent it with.

As I shuffled toward the spiralizer of the 2016 job hunt, I was sensing I might not be made of the right stuff. I don't just mean physically, though that's impossible to sift out of conversations about belonging, especially in the law. I mean I was starting to doubt whether I had the mind or constitution to be a lawyer. The more I learned about the world of practice, the less I thought I might be able to handle it. I wasn't unique in my delayed recognition: In the fog of legal education, the peaks and depressions of the professional landscape are known to be well-hidden until the moment your body breaks against them. But back then, I was still committed to making it work despite my doubts. I scrolled through dozens of law firm websites, past grinning white people who loved the hundred-hour work week, and made a list of firms I would apply to. Every website had a section devoted to inclusion. If I knew a student who'd summered there, I cross-checked the equity statements with someone who'd seen it in the flesh. The answer for how the two aligned was, uniformly, "terribly."

I wasn't particularly surprised—after all, I knew what the inside of a classroom looked like—but I'd been hoping for something to hook into in a field that remained stubbornly alien to me. There was also something mercenary in asking: my grades from the previous semester had died on the curve and I was looking for any way to stand out. Not by selling myself as a diversity hire, that's gross, but by demonstrating that the firm and I shared a commitment to a core value. As I said, I knew what the inside of a law classroom looked like and the devil's advocacy that took place inside of it; how conversations often cut away social realities in the service of pure logic. How many of those people, I wagered, were going to snap employers to attention by citing the undeniable importance of diversity in their cover letters? Six years later, I'm scandalized by such cynical use of *diversity* as a skeleton key. It belies a ruthlessness I didn't believe myself capable of, even as it's a logical extension of what courts and corporations have inflated the word to mean. But it also matched my past forays into discussing the topic, which had ended much the same as my chats with upper-year law students: with shrugged shoulders and an agreement that things looked grim.

In law school, the second-year summer job gets talked about like it's the fulcrum of a young career. This can be true, but it isn't dogmatically so—though the nature of the recruiting process makes it look like it is. In the fall of second year, law students submit to a whirlwind job hunt known as on-campus interviews (OCIs). Over the course of a week, students sit for brief discussions with employers that, if they go well, unlock a highly formalized courting process: a longer interview at the law firm, a dinner on the town with the partners, perhaps a cocktail hour where you bat your lashes and tell a firm that they're your "first choice." The frenzy culminates on Call Day at 8 a.m., which is exactly what it sounds like: if an employer wants you bad, that is when they call to say so. If multiple employers want you bad, it's when they call, too. There are less terrifying ways to secure a summer gig. There's basic networking, or working at one of the school's affiliated legal clinics, or applying for faculty research assistantships. But it's a huge load off if you manage to score a position by November of your second year. Also, most of those other jobs pay peanuts in comparison. As a result, the pressure to get hired during this cycle steams off students so thickly, it seems to alter the AQI of the surrounding area. Even if your career goals don't involve full-service business firms (the bulk of participating employers), why would you waste a clear shot at paying down six figures of debt?

Though my professional aims were already prickling toward the public interest rather than corporate law, I set about molding myself to fit various workplaces. I was especially keen to apply to firms in

New York, which often hired students from Toronto—the idea of living in New York seemed like it might redeem a lot of my suffering. An upper-year student had given me a good piece of advice: Look up each firm's recent big cases and mention them in my cover letters. It implied that I'd done basic research, maybe even harbored personal interest, and that I wasn't just blasting all of Big Law with a plea to stem the hemorrhage of tuition (which is exactly what I, and others, were doing). I'm sure citing recent cases was low-hanging fruit and employers saw right through it, but as I've said, with my transcript, I needed to score points where I could. My grades were straight average—basically the minimum they give you for paying thirty grand, showing up to the exam, and regurgitating the shit you've memorized. I'd nearly broken myself second semester, but when you're graded on a proportional curve in a class full of geniuses, you don't get extra credit for things like "breaking yourself."

My cover letters, sent in flurries to firms in New York City and Toronto, professed to many different "particular areas of interest." I dropped classmates' names like marbles. I skimmed and quoted cases that the firms had been involved in and hoped I wasn't misinterpreting the principle the way I kept doing on exams. In the letter that felt most original, I employed my diversity strategy. I'd noticed, on the firm's list of cases, one that was about affirmative action—a rare spot of real interest for me among cases on corporate mergers and pharmaceutical patents. They'd written an amicus brief, which I read only enough of to make sure they weren't on the racist side. Then I wrote, prissily, in my cover letter: "I am also excited by your firm's commitment to diversity, a cause for which I have been an advocate in my work as an actor. Of particular interest to me was the recent amicus brief in *Fisher v. University of Texas at Austin*." *Fisher* was basically the 2016 iteration of *Bakke* (though I didn't know about old Allan at the time). A white girl had brought the latest challenge to race-sensitive admissions because her grades weren't good enough for UT.

I've spent the years since believing I'd avoided the diversity tack altogether; that I'd written it off as too charged, or too crassly opportunist. I kept up that delusion until I was reading over old applications while writing this essay and was arrested by the reference to *Fisher*. And maybe the firm did see through me—citing the case didn't work and I didn't get the interview. But I also didn't sue anyone for discrimination.

Though I came up empty in my pitches for New York, I scored seven meetings on the Toronto circuit. The first-round interviews were split across two days and took place at the local public library, which felt like a betrayal by the library. The unimaginative but accurate metaphor for OCIs is speed dating, in which prospective hires rotate through cloth-draped cubicles in fifteen-minute increments, pump the hands of a few associates, and make glorified small talk. You can't cover that much substantive ground in fifteen minutes; they'll mostly just look at your transcript and ask you trivial things about yourself. More of the law-specific stuff comes if you make it to the infirm stage. (For me, the entire OCI process felt like one long, drawn-out in-firm stage.) What they're assessing, at this first checkpoint, is basically your vibe.

On the day of the interviews, law students were penned in a small back room, thick with the funk of armpit, with a door that periodically opened at the ding of an invisible bell. With each cycle, a new batch of bodies was released into a large, high-ceilinged room, crosshatched by black curtains that formed the identical interview pods. You had about a minute to find your cubicle; maps abounded, as did prayers that you peeped behind the right curtain. Between dates, you milled around bovinely in the back, picked at cold pastries, and tried not to make eye contact, lest someone else start fanning the coals of your panic. My written talking points included "race and the criminal justice system," listed for an interview with the prosecutor's office, which is a hilarious bit of self-sabotage. Did

I think I was going to reform the system in a fifteen-minute interview? Most of my chats were anodyne in the harmless way where both sides silently agree there's not enough attraction to pursue. In my most promising interview, with a midsize criminal defense firm, I spent most of my minutes answering questions about my work as a voice actor. The two recruiters seemed to find my job a hilarious bit of trivia that was far more fascinating than my transcript, which was fine by me. There was very forced laughter on both sides. Somehow, I managed to spin that into an in-firm interview and, later, a dinner.

The dinner was closer to the end of the week, after my other six interviews had ended with a polite exchange of thank-you notes and then radio silence. It took place the night of November 8, 2016, so we were all a little distracted. I'd had a small panic attack earlier in the evening, but it was about the fact that I'd reached third base with a firm rather than the election. Everyone met at an Italian restaurant just outside Toronto's financial district, our party of law students and lawyers numbering around ten. We were seated near a TV that flashed blue and red; everyone around the table was, at least vocally, With Her. The waiter proffered an aperitif with a berry split on the rim; it mashed against my cheek every time I took a sip. A senior partner asked for a red wine that he liked—"Tell them it's for me" was all the instruction he gave the waiter—and though I'd rank that night among the worst of my life, that nameless wine remains the single best I've ever had. When the senior partner placed his fingertips on the base of his glass and swirled the liquid around in tight little circles, the students around the table mirrored the gesture like he'd ordered us to do it in sync. As the night wore on, he launched into the story of how he built his firm. Starting out as a young lawyer, he said, he'd noticed an explosion of police-defense cases and cannily followed the money.

"I can only imagine that part of your practice will keep growing," said another student. There were four of us being assessed at this dinner, and this girl was about to nail it. So was the guy with political connections who was matching the partners scotch for scotch. "I mean, with all the scrutiny on police these days—especially south of the border." The partner agreed. I'd hoped law school would make me sharper, quicker to object to injustice when I saw it, but I was so horrified, I couldn't speak. I received a polite and relieving rejection email the next day.

Though I didn't get a summer job through OCIs, I had a comparatively easy go on the nightmare ride. The annual recruitment feature, published by the law student paper, tells a darker story, one that's more revealing of the profession's endemic and aggressive whiteness. After crunching the numbers submitted by participating firms and candidates in 2016, the piece shares select anonymized student responses. The anecdotes are often just a line or two, but that's all you need to understand the scene: racist jokes at cocktail parties; dismissal of DEI initiatives (a lawyer called them unnecessary because "no one would even think about being racist" in Canada); a cameo by the diversity-hire trope ("One interviewer made a comment about how it's a shame I'm not a visible minority").

During this period, and in law school more generally, I felt a shift in my understanding of what I asked of institutions and what they expected of me. The language of diversity presupposes that fixing the external world is possible, at least theoretically. The law, for all its faults, does not abide that story. Improvement isn't about redistributing power but perfecting an internal circuit. Think of *Bakke*, the strict legal test that got a white man into med school on a technicality—the case was about striving for false balance within a system rather than realigning it. At no point would the Court have considered, as a factor, a Black student protesting outside UC Davis, one who didn't have funds to write the MCAT at all because the state has spent centuries preventing Black families from building wealth.

Being trained to think like a lawyer in class, or act like a lawyer at dinner, was a constant reminder that the train chugging steadily toward enlightenment was rolling over piles of bodies. Obviously, it doesn't read that way to every farm boy, but to me, there was something instructive in getting the regular memo. It's part of why I left the law, albeit a relatively small part. More meaningfully, it clarified all the times I'd been pulled into a room to talk about diversity as both physician and cure, and it shaped my attitude toward all the rooms yet to come: the institution is not your home, it does not care about you, and it is not your job to fix it. To some people this will sound obvious; to others, harsh. But I wasn't born knowing it and I still find value in saying it, especially during a time when, for a number of organizations, "fix us" has become item one on the agenda.

EVEN THOUGH IT'S not our job to fix them, and even though the tools of language are cracked and dull, the work is still important. If you're the only one in the room, it's your job to get somebody else in there with you. I'm not going to dig up the foundations or even repaint the walls, but I *can* wedge open the door. This is my personal target, but I've learned the many ways white management may try to shift it. It's easy, as Ahmed writes in *On Being Included*, to become "the diversity person" when you're already considered "diverse." You embody a brighter future as soon as you enter the space.

It's well documented that the work of equity committees falls unevenly on Black and racialized employees. Hiring a consultant is expensive—diversity work is a multi-billion-dollar industry—but if a company has successfully squared away its diversity hires, they can get the fix for free. Though ad hoc committees alone are not enough, companies aren't always willing to dip into the pot to hire an external DEI consultant. Kicking up a fuss about workplace whiteness might get you marked in an interview, but all is fair once you've been told to do so by your boss. The very serious function of racism may be distraction, but this is considered a worthwhile one. Even if we value the duty and believe in the outcome, it cheapens the work when it's framed as "for the good of the company" and not "for the good of the people shut out of it."

The process is long and slow and piecemeal, badly codified and largely unprotected. The ghost of reverse discrimination still haunts the language of equal opportunity. In the United States, one variation of the clause in job postings goes something like this: "qualified applicants will receive consideration *without regard to* race, national origin, religion, age, color, sex, sexual orientation, gender identity, disability, or protected veteran status," emphasis mine. Sometimes the language is more lenient, but it isn't always. If the Supreme Court decides more permissive policy is unconstitutional, then the burden on diversity workers will only grow heavier. In Canada, the hiring provisos leave less room for a reverse-discrimination reading, but ghosts can pass through keyholes of any size. Who's going to get saddled with the exorcism—the one Black woman on your board of directors? Stanley from *The Office*? For as long as they spend begging their white co-workers to join hands, to come together and banish the apparition, the lone staffer of color will never feel like a real part of the corporation's family. But their boss must have already known that from years of tuning in to office sitcoms.

This Time It's Personal

My first-ever stab at a personal essay is saved on my hard drive as "personal essay.docx." Clearly, I only planned to hit it once. Getting serious about the form seemed like a bad idea; in 2016, people talked about the genre like the circus had packed up and gone. Writers had eaten fire and swallowed swords and bared every conceivable crevice. Sure, you might be a bona fide freak, but even so, how were you going to outdo what had already been done? Admitting I wanted to try felt gauche and possibly a route to grievous bodily harm. While none of these fears were well-founded, they tainted the air enough that I held my breath. I also had my own private doubts about the essay. Hunger made me seek out collections in bookshops; vicarious shame made me slap covers shut. No matter how great a writer's life seemed to be, everything always hurt when they pressed on it, like the joke about going to the doctor with a broken finger. At the same time, I envied the anthropological clarity these writers brought to their pain. They seemed to perceive their lives and the forces that shaped them more keenly than I did mine. I would try it, I decided. Just once. In secret.

The essay I wrote is about growing up a speck in the eye of a white suburb, a story I'd been raised to believe was flecked with prejudice, but not infected by it. As a child, I was taught to see discrimination as patterned only insofar as it acted upon large groups of people, and even then, the context was usually a brief history lesson. What happened to me in school and on the street was portrayed more like lightning—scorching, sure, but also random and discrete. A personal essay seemed like the right vehicle to collect all the counterevidence. My desire to make sense of myself and my story was genuine. But my aims were also mercenary: I wasn't pressing on these memories because it hurt so good to do it, but because they seemed like the kind of thing that got published online. Not that I was ever planning to do anything like that.

The grievances amounted to five thousand words titled, after Zora Neale Hurston, "A Sharp White Background." (My sample size had taught me that subtlety was not required.) Whole paragraphs came easy, the process feeling frictionless the way an art can when you don't know enough of its rules to be hard on yourself. Writing, as I knew it, was dense and heavy work, and fiction had taught me the labor it takes to look graceful. But the lightness of this essay's composition felt all out of scale with the heft of the result, like I'd been playing in the sand and unearthed a buried skeleton, grisly and inevitable and so near the surface it seemed like a health risk. I hadn't constructed something so much as extracted it, and now that it sat steaming and exposed to the air, I was horrified by the pit it had come from.

Had I really been carrying around this gaping sense of woundedness for my entire life? Was I in danger of bleeding out? Worse, was this the deeply unfunny vibe I gave off as a person? All things considered, I thought my childhood had been pretty good! And yet the essay inflected my character with something noble, too; the idea that, as I moved through the world, I silently nurtured this yawning hurt by virtue of who I was. I thought I'd sucked the poison out, spat it into some nice sentences, and that was where the story would end. Especially since even more people, by then, were saying that the personal essay had straight-up *died*. But then, a few weeks later, I had a thought about how something else that happened in my life had been shaped by painful feelings of difference. Then another. My relationship to memory had suddenly become the trick where the clown, in mixed wonder and dread, keeps pulling knotted handkerchiefs out of his mouth. How far down do they go—are they crammed in his trachea? Curled in his stomach?

Six years later, I'm not horrified, nor even really surprised, that this was the tune that emerged when I tried to sing the inaugural song of myself. After all, I'd been keeping an eye on the writers at the vanguard, seeing what kind of behavior got rewarded, and I've always been a canny mimic. My essay struck a set of poses common to a certain type of personal story: an implied sameness between being racialized and feeling existential pain, anxiety over an imagined failure to embody "authenticity," seeing one's reflection in popular media as a political endgame. Though these are very much tropes, they also gave me a way to express something that felt, at the time, both vivid and true. (They didn't, small mercy, get me published, at least not that first time.) I've encountered versions of this essay many times in the years since. I've read and reread it, assigned it, rejected it. I've seen it castigated by satires and complaints, but also summoned by submissions calls and expensive book deals. I've written it a few more times, too, though often not on purpose. Various market forces guide writers into producing this kind of piece; sometimes, writers guide themselves. That there's an ongoing appetite for it says something essential about the reading public and the language we use to tell the story of selfhood.

Using firsthand experience as a political hook has become a staple of digital publishing. Confessionals of the past, like "My Gynecologist Found a Ball of Cat Hair in My Vagina"—a viral *xoJane* piece from 2015 that is often cited as the trend's peak—no longer cut it if they aren't yoked to something like "And Here's What That Taught Me about White Supremacy." I'm describing a specific type of personal writing here; not the inevitable outcome of putting yourself on paper but a version manufactured by a certain set of circumstances, like guilty white newsrooms and the churn of the internet. The demand for these accounts falls most heavily on writers from marginalized backgrounds. Several linked premises scaffold the persistence and popularity of these pieces: that one's personal story should bloom around suffering; that suffering is inextricable from being alive and minoritized; that giving such pain a platform is inherently moral; and, perhaps most significantly, that consuming it is evidence of a higher goodness. In other words, it's a cycle in which everyone is complicit.

Selfhood, as a subject, has always been a wellspring for writers— not least the tradition of Black and racialized essayists who wrote their personal histories into a world that denied their humanity. But, as digital media seeks its own fixes to historical problems, tales of anguished subjectivity have become a new boon—a quick hit of empathy meant to confirm that to be both "other" and alive is, inevitably and spectacularly, to hurt.

THE PERSONAL-ESSAY genre has had a famously rough stretch of years, and critiques of the form don't go over well. In 2017, Jia Tolentino published a widely misread piece in *The New Yorker*, "The Personal-Essay Boom Is Over." The article would later be cited as a wholesale takedown of the *I*, but Tolentino's target is more precise than that. She focuses on a "specific sort of ultra-confessional essay" that used to strike the internet in frequent flashes, illuminating the lives and minds of normal people—usually women—at their most shocking and vulnerable. In a media economy of gouged editorial budgets and slashed ad sales, scandalous personal stories were a free lunch: they didn't take the time or money of hard reporting, and they tapped into a prurient impulse that scored the pageviews publications needed to survive. Editors thirsted for suffering and writers curved to meet their desires; "the online personal essay," writes Tolentino, "began to harden into a form defined by identity and adversity." The adversity of the type she describes, though, was never all that bad—minor gynecological snafus, racist thoughts in yoga class—and this frivolity put a stamp on the essay's shelf life. The bubble had been inflating for a while—in 2015, *Slate*'s Laura Bennett coined the phrase "first-person industrial complex"—but by late 2016, Tolentino says, it did what bubbles always do eventually. After Trump was elected, "the personal [was] no longer political in quite the same way," and that brand of exposure accordingly vanished from the web.

Personal essayists took Tolentino's critique, well, personally. Several responses seized on her observations about the form—often fairly neutral ones, like "women do it" (because female-interest sites are underfunded and the social conditions of women's lives can be abominable)—and recast them as attacks. No matter how trivial the subject, the rebuttals went, women sharing their experiences at all is a radical thing, and to dare call its politics into question was the same as telling them to shut up. It's a slippery slope, a response in *Salon* desperately submitted, from muzzling "messy storytelling" to canceling Beyoncé's *Lemonade*. Two years prior, Bennett's *Slate* piece had met similar allegations of sexist dog-whistling. Among a set of responses published in the *Guardian*, an *xoJane* editor insisted women's stories "often reflect the feminist maxim that the personal is political," and to suggest that there might be something exploitive in splashing a novice writer's trauma across the internet "denies [adult women] an awful lot of agency." This wasn't egotism; it was radical feminism. (This is exactly the kind of false equivalence—aesthetic mess spun into political gold by way of extreme vulnerability—the ultra-confessional essay loves to perform, which is what made me suspicious of it in the first place. Literary form is not patriarchal violence.)

This was a white women's fight. A call to raise the bar on the form's political content—especially when our world is an intensifying house of horrors, for some people more rapidly than others—wasn't an attack on feminine speech, nor a fresh axis of oppression. Beyoncé is not threatened by the squabbles of literary Twitter, though it says a lot that these writers felt justified comparing their hot takes to *Lemonade*. But humming under their defensive responses is an understandable, if overwrought, anxiety about legitimacy. The first-person essay comes saddled with accusations of artlessness and narcissism, and in history as in the present, you're likelier to attract those critiques if you're not a cisgender man.

Whenever anything gets democratized—like how the first-person essay leveled literary ground for writers of marginalized backgrounds and genders—people cry that equitable access has cheapened its value. In 1905, Virginia Woolf lamented "The Decay of Essay Writing," chiding a public so enamored of its newfound literacy that it was cranking out takes better left unsaid. Though robust nonfiction sections and frequent splashy book deals suggest that we've moved past most of the stigma, a trace of it has never really gone away. Editors, writers, and a certain type of reader still balk at the suggestion of kinship between their icy intellectual worlds and that vomit-like, uncouth thing people do online. A cottage industry of novelists will churn out angry op-eds if you hint that their book contains a whiff of autobiography. Critics who see first-person pronouns in reviews retort that they "don't care about your life." This seemed, for a little while, like it would be the personal essay's resting place: a form that was allowed to exist, but begrudgingly; a thing we'd avert our eyes from if somebody suddenly announced they had to do it. But the form has also proved nimble enough to metabolize complaint and evolve a new strain. It's funny, in retrospect, that its death ever really seemed to be on the table. Some impulses run too deep to root out: the anxious urge to tell the story of ourselves. The prurient hunger for an aperture into the lives of others not like us. The confirmation of certain insidious assumptions about the lives and feelings of those "others." The personal essay has proved itself a vehicle uniquely suited to these transactions.

"The first-person boom," Laura Bennett writes in *Slate*, "has had one significant benefit: There's more of a market for underrepresented viewpoints than ever." All you needed, credentials-wise, was for some minorly shocking stuff to have happened to you and a willingness to spill it. With its low barriers to entry, the personal essay could bend toward justice. This is a small and rather counterintuitive miracle: that time and goodwill will passively breed diversity is how a lot of institutions *hope* they'll become less homogenous, but sitting around doing nothing isn't actually supposed to work. Soraya Roberts, in a piece published on *thewalrus.ca*, surveyed the post-2016 genre and agreed with Tolentino that gross-out and deeply revealing material were no longer political enough to survive. But that argument, as Roberts saw it, was "looking the wrong way"—the voices at the new vanguard, like Roxane Gay, Samantha Irby, and Scaachi Koul, had given fresh life to the form. The personal essay "isn't dead," Roberts wrote, "it's just no longer white."

More than other literary genres, Roberts continued, first-person pieces gave underrepresented writers the space to "[interrogate] the culture that refused to recognize them." But this new visibility was a mixed blessing. For a number of minoritized writers, especially those without book deals or staff jobs and looking to snag their first byline, the minorly shocking stuff that happened to them was, often, life in their own bodies and the violence they were met with because of it. Writing in *The New Republic*, Stacia L. Brown was less sanguine about how the form slurps the marrow of identity: "when women of color write about their personal experiences, they're asked to make a cottage industry of their encounters with racism and sexism." Writing on lighter subjects, or edgier, sexier ones, remained the provenance of white women. Cat Marnell might get a reported six-figure book deal for chronicling her sex life and drug use, but a Black woman would publish "one successful, gut-wrenching piece somewhere, and then hear 'no' . . . until [she'd] exploit personal trauma" ad infinitum.

I came to this world as a writer of few bylines and fewer connections. I had no concept of journalism as a thing one "got into," like fisticuffs or Bitcoin. The only person I knew of who was connected to the local paper was whoever chucked it at the houses on our block, and that person was usually my little brother on his paper route. Magazines were things you sent away for and, when they got there, piled them in a basket by the toilet. Years earlier, I'd met a handful of journalists through my voice-over work, which had made me a local curiosity as a ten-year-old with a weird job, and which also meant the paper that thumped against our door sometimes had my face in it. This was my only exposure to the actual work of journalism till about fifteen years later. Reporters would come to my parents' house, or call me on the phone, or take my dad and me to dinner, and ask questions that caused me intense anxiety—serious, world-bending queries I didn't have the answers to but knew I had to bullshit, because otherwise, what were they going to say about me in their articles? I spun many long, lyrical fictions in answer to things like *what are your plans for the future?* or *do you have advice for other kids trying to break into the industry?* or *how would you describe this salmon sashimi?* But when I picked up the paper to read the final, published pieces—slim, printed columns that referred to me, with beguiling gravity, as simply "Isen"— it was as if they'd remixed the recording. I was sure I'd gone into more detail about the sashimi than just saying it was "delectable."

This was the extent of my education in media when I started pitching in my twenties. Unlike those early enigmas of the local paper, the internet felt different. The inner workings of an elaborate and fast-moving system were revealing themselves to me with what felt like complete transparency. Seeing who and what was getting published, I felt the pull of permission, even of invitation, to become a part of something vital. I locked onto the frequency and began to flay myself on the page.

An essay could be about anything—books, music, cartoons,

films—and I'd always be able to relate it to a time when I'd felt marginalized or underrepresented. I could tell that editors liked it. Sometimes they pressed on the bruise harder than was comfortable, but I would let it go, thicken my skin and amend the sentences. After all, I'd been the one to bring it up first. Around then, toward the end of law school, I started thinking about writing as a thing I could do for money, which may have brought a certain ruthlessness to the way I carved myself up. Ditto after graduating without a job. But I was also truly exhilarated to be doing that kind of work. It felt weighty, politically significant. I'd wanted to break into the world of online writing and they'd let me. I also felt like I was beginning to understand myself more clearly—the exact sense of clarity I'd envied when I started reading other people's personal essays. I'd imagined my own inner workings would take more time to parse, but the mechanism was disarmingly simple. One key seemed to unlock every door. There was no mystery or discontinuity or threat, in the world or in me, that could not be explained, clarified, or even neutralized by the phrase "As a woman of color . . ."

I believed, at least at first, that this was agency. At its best, that's what the personal-essay economy does: It gives writers a way to reclaim stories and moments that life has wrenched away from them. At its worst, it might push writers to express a pain that comes off looking worse than how they really feel. Or it might become the broken-finger problem, where pressing on a thing that hurts becomes your whole refrain.

This is what happened to me. Eventually, reading back my published work gave me the same doubled sense of standing outside myself I'd first felt with "A Sharp White Background"—*who is she, what's her problem, where the hell's her sense of humor?* Every argument got routed toward the same conclusion even if I set out to end up elsewhere, like someone had flipped the switch on a track when I wasn't looking. (Sometimes, that someone was me.)

I don't blame any of the editors I worked with during this period; I think I had to transgress the boundary of my comfort before I understood the extent of the pain scale. But I also think the literary ecosystem is set up such that, if you venture slightly further in the direction of expressing pain, you might find more taken from you than you were willing to give. And yet, to a well-meaning editor, and also an imagined reader, I can see how the final pieces didn't look much further along the axis than my first drafts had. They thought they were just cleaning up my copy, helping me speak my truth. Maybe I'd even set myself up for it, tracing the contours of a story so familiar, other people knew how to finish my sentences better than I did.

A WRITER'S SELFHOOD may be the subject of a piece, but it might also be a qualification to speak on a topic other than themselves. Their body might lend the story a fresher news peg, or gild it with insider knowledge, because they have literal skin in the game. This is the principle underlying *Vox*'s "First Person" section, in which personal stories help advance the outlet's mission to explain the news: "A retired Secret Service agent can illuminate the agency's problems in ways a news story might miss," the description of the page says, or a woman "with an anxiety disorder can explain her experience in a way even the best statistics will hide." But casting the writer as spokesperson can smack more obviously of tokenization, like this piece published in the same vertical: "I'm a black ex-cop, and this is the real truth about race and policing." Writers usually don't come up with their own headlines, and I'm sure this author saw and lived awful things on the job. But policing is not some sort of niche, the-personal-is-political topic. This is facile engagement with an elemental social problem while saving the time and money of having a staff writer report it out. The outlet keeps the budget, the writer gets his byline, the story gets its stakes and tension, and readers can avoid engaging more deeply since they now know "the real truth."

In digital media, this reactive story commissioning is a common move. Cord Jefferson published "The Racism Beat" in 2014, about the emotional tax of being asked to file copy every time "something bad happen[s] to a black person." The beat is grimly circuitous: Black writers are "compelled on a consistent basis to defend [their] claim to dignity" because they're writing for an audience that needs to be regularly reminded of it. Laura Bennett cites "The Racism Beat" as one sign of a bright future for the first-person industrial complex. She reads it as a model of writing about oneself that's "gripping and sensitive and that sheds light on broader sociopolitical issues." Jefferson's essay is all of those things, absolutely. But it's also about the punishing work of constantly having that type of writing annexed to stories of violence.

For some writers, this labor can be the price of admission into the literary sphere. Morgan Jerkins tells a story that's similar, in certain ways, to Jefferson's. In *Lenny Letter*, she describes the way she found her voice as a writer. Coverage of the Ferguson uprisings had brought a push for more Black voices in newsrooms, and white editors saw Jerkins's tweets about Michael Brown's murder. They reached out to assign her "stories about black suffering and trauma." Jerkins describes, very frankly, the way she "capitalized on this moment . . . as a career opportunity," grinding out pitches with such militancy that her inbox seemed to ping with each new incident of police brutality. People were suddenly paying attention to her and her work. Though she relished her newfound power, the same piece describes how she also started having nightmares about bodily violence, burnt out shortly thereafter, and had to rethink her relationship to her work.

Black suffering has always been a form of North American entertainment; now, outlets can also call upon a version of it as a political necessity. On some level, this is just how life operates online. As our digital selves steadily supplant our physical ones, speech becomes easily conflated with action. Expressing an opinion on Twitter, or retweeting an essay on the struggle of being a Black woman, becomes a stand-in for actually doing anything to change the systems that give rise to it. You don't have to worry about transforming social conditions for Black women if you can just pick one voice and amplify it ad infinitum.

Maybe here's where I should admit how uncomfortable I am with the way the word *identity* gets used to describe personal writing, or any creative work at all. I've often heard people say that an essay or book is "about identity," the way you'd say that a text is "about millennials having bad sex in Brooklyn" or "about life in the endgame of climate apocalypse." Those other examples tell you something about the subject matter. Not so with identity. *Identity* isn't a description but a judgment. It's an unfair bit of shorthand that filters a work's contents—which may or may not engage with subjects like race and class and gender—through a tiny keyhole: the ways in which its writer has been marginalized. It doesn't matter what they say, or how they say it—what they're *really* talking about is who they are.

To be fair, some people are okay with being interpreted this way. The language of social justice circulates more freely than ever, in casual conversation as in literary writing. People invoke their identities, with varying degrees of cynicism, as the crux of their arguments on the page and off. Some artists *want* "as a person of x background" to be the bottom line of all their work. Some artists want to express, for the leering reader, the truths of "what it means" to inhabit their body. But *identity* is not a catchall category for any art by anyone from any underrepresented group—even if that work is alert to how power works in the world. That description doesn't say anything about the work itself, only how the work is perceived: *This must be the unmediated data of your life. That must have been so hard. You must be in so much pain.*

THERE ARE OTHER ways to tell personal stories—the story of what it means to be different, or the story of selfhood at all. The form has deeper roots than the starving digital media economy. "I am not tragically colored," Zora Neale Hurston wrote in 1928. "I do not belong to the sobbing school of Negrohood who hold that nature somehow has given them a low-down dirty deal and whose feelings are all but about it." Her essay, "How It Feels to Be Colored Me," narrates the fateful splitting of consciousness recounted by many Black writers. Until age thirteen, Hurston lived in the all-Black town of Eatonville, Florida. White people would ride through sometimes, but only in passing; accordingly, our narrator was simply "Zora." But when she leaves the town to attend school in Jacksonville, Hurston is enclosed in a menagerie of white people, a world that turns her "fast brown." The essay toggles between her two selves and two ways of seeing. "I do not always feel colored," Hurston writes; "I feel most colored when I am thrown against a sharp white background."

There's a deliberate buoyancy to her tone, a bravado so playful it turns dangerous: "No, I do not weep at the world—I'm too busy sharpening my oyster knife." Even though my earliest attempts at the personal essay definitely *did* weep at the world, Hurston's pose also feels familiar to me, the bared-teeth determination to prove you're not the thing everyone expects you to be—in her case, anguished. But anguish, too, can be a fitting register. Twenty-five years earlier, W.E.B. Du Bois had related the same moment of recognition in a different key. In "Of Our Spiritual Strivings," the first essay in *The Souls of Black Folk*, he offers a set piece from his New England childhood, in which students in his schoolhouse exchanged cards with one another. A tall white girl rejects Du Bois's proffered card, a gesture that jars his understanding of himself: "it dawned upon me with a certain suddenness," he writes, "that I was different from the others . . . shut out from the world by a vast veil." While Hurston delights in lifting and dropping the veil depending on the company she keeps, Du Bois has "no desire to tear [it] down." For him, the epiphany of his difference is fixed and final.

Hurston and Du Bois articulate the same experience—of realizing that one is set apart by virtue of being Black—very differently. Hurston's rendering crackles and whirls; with Du Bois, it's like something's clanged shut. The instant of confronting (or more often, being violently confronted by) one's difference has attracted a lot of treatment in writing. This makes sense: finding that tear in the social world, running your hand along it, and crossing to the other side is a line you can only really traverse one way. Putting it on the page establishes a link between the essayist and a lineage of Black writing, whose earliest progenitors—in speeches, pamphlets, and slave narratives—defended their right to be free. Barred from public life, the private was a powerful space in which they could claim authority.

When I first tried to write this experience for myself, I hadn't read either of these essays, though I'd encountered a few examples that were trying to do something similar. But I learned very quickly that the sensation can be hard to describe without draining the prose, or even one's entire persona on the page, of joy. This makes sense: when this moment happens in real life, it usually hurts. Even Hurston swaps in a pun in lieu of representing the instant she transforms ("When I disembarked from the river-boat at Jacksonville, [Zora] was no more. It seemed that I had suffered a sea change"), a joke I read as a minor deflection. It can be difficult, in other words, not to figure the moment as agonizing. Yet, this same agony plays into the prurient itch to know what it's like to be, in Du Bois's words, "a problem."

Contemporary audiences, I'd argue, have come to expect those beats: the problem, the pain, the difference, the otherness. These scenes of subjection have become part of the news cycle and tend to spike in times of crisis. Recall what Laura Bennett said back in 2015: not that the personal-essay economy contains more of a *movement to support* or an *interest in elevating* underrepresented voices, but that it has more of a *market* for them. Her terminology is accurate, and market trends are fickle. In the wake of highly public incidents of anti-Black racism and police violence, this type of essay is often retooled to meet a fresh wave of demand. The internet gets an influx of takes like "I Took My First Date to the Black Lives Matter Protest" (*Refinery29*, taken down swiftly); "What It's Like to Be Biracial in the Age of Black Lives Matter" (*Cosmopolitan*, later retitled but the cache remembers); "I Spent 35 Years Trying to Convince the World (And Myself) That I'm White" (*Huffington Post*). White writers get in on it, too: "My Wife Is Black. My Son Is Biracial. But White Supremacy Lives Inside Me" (*WBUR*); "What the Black Lives Matter Movement Has Taught Me About My Whiteness" (*O, The Oprah Magazine*, written by its deputy editor); "I'm Moving My Family to Canada to Save My Black Son from America" (*Cosmo* again, and also, that won't work).

Grabby headlines aside, the problem isn't with the pieces themselves. This is relatively standard personal-essay fare, and I don't want to rule out the possibility that pitching and writing stories like these are part of the way some people process. The problem is that, amid the call to "amplify Black voices" that tears across publishing every few years, *these* were the stories outlets sought as proof that Black lives mattered. The headlines echo the voyeuristic itch of the first-person industrial complex. There's an anthropological curiosity in their framing, redirecting the reader's attention from a broken system to the individualized suffering of being Black while inside of it. The only ones who need dispatches about *what it's like* to live in a certain body in the age of Black Lives Matter are white people.

Now, when these essays explode across the internet, I'm on the other side, in the editor's chair. Despite my prior view of journalism as a smooth-walled, sealed thing, I was lucky to find a few entry points. Pitching and writing personal essays had been one of them; a contract as a fact-checker was another. Now, years later, I've become someone responsible for handling the delicate substance of people's lives. Writers hand me a slice of their most vulnerable selves, and it's my job and my privilege to make sure the editorial process never approaches the pain of the thing they may be writing about. In journalism, depending on the kind of outlet where you work, you may also be assigned the coarser task of predicting and catering to the audience's appetite. After something like a highly public incident of racist violence, it takes no skill to read the wind. It's obvious what people want to read, because it's the same thing that people always want to read, except with sudden-onset feverish intensity.

In journalism, as in other cultural industries, so many sins get committed under the sign of finding the broadest possible audience. What I wouldn't give, at times like those, for Zora's oyster knife.

THE PROBLEM WITH creating an audience hungry for pain is that you have to feed it constantly. Even as more writers reject these expectations for being too restrictive, readers and critics still rely on them—so much so that they'll even read suffering into work that's manifestly about something else. We may have moved past a blanket dismissal of all personal essayists as artless hacks, but the standard of proof is still punishingly high if you're part of an underrepresented group. No matter their aesthetic or formal achievements, a writer might get asked why their work doesn't hit the beats the reader has come to expect. Worse, the writer may not even get the dubious grace of that question in the first place. The work will simply be reframed in a way that serves the reader's appetite. This is the "about identity" judgment taken to harmful extremes—the assumption that work by nonwhite writers must be about trauma and little else. Nobody stops to consider what the writer might actually be trying to do, or whether they might be doing those things well.

The 2019 essay collection *A Mind Spread Out on the Ground*, by Haudenosaunee writer Alicia Elliott, was subject to such treatment. Elliott's book weaves personal narrative with a wide-ranging analysis of colonialism's effects on contemporary Indigenous life in North

America. The collection received a positive review in the *New York Times*, but the publication presented it as a very different book from the one I've just described: as "a broad-strokes map of Native brokenness, crisscrossed by rivers of blood," and a "searing cry to stanch the bleeding." The gap here seems bigger than your average interpretive license. Elliott addressed the review on Twitter, noting how she felt it unimaginatively cast her book as "trauma porn" and that it made no effort to talk about craft or "the innovative ways [she] engaged with the essay." Instead, the writer drew on clichés about the supposedly inherent tragedy of Indigenous life. The risk of being read this way is so high, some writers anticipate it before it even happens. Kiese Laymon, whose memoir *Heavy* was one of the most acclaimed books of 2018, told BuzzFeed that he was "aware that the content [of *Heavy*] would open it up to accusations of titillation and trauma porn." But Laymon, a writer who has more than proved his capacity for craft, felt the need to assert that his depiction of Black life is "still art."

The presumption of artlessness even came up in the way that people, bless them, talked about *this* book when they learned of its eventual existence: nervously joking about the cameos they'd make in a book about lip service, unable to envision a final product that wasn't born of weeping into a diary or tapping a vein. While there's nothing wrong with dropping something straight out of your life and into your art, that's never been the kind of writer I am. I value rigor and discipline as inherently moral. I distrust anyone who claims they can't be constrained by the tyranny of form, because form is what I worship. But because of who I am and what I write about, I face the uphill battle to prove I know my way around a sentence.

An entire alternative critical vocabulary has mushroomed up in order to avoid talking about how minoritized writers use craft or style. Such language—words like *urgent, raw,* and *visceral* are commonly called upon—tends to emphasize how great of a job the work is doing simply by existing, rather than how successful it is (or is not) in accomplishing its goals. These appraisals grade works on a scale of political efficacy rather than aesthetic merit, where "political efficacy" means something like "is by or about someone who isn't white" and "makes me feel like a better person for having read." In the *New York Times Magazine*, Lauren Oyler notes the rise of *necessary* as a critical descriptor, and the dully predictable tendency to throw the word at artists from marginalized backgrounds. The label casts their work as a thing "that would have happened regardless of creative agency," a mass that flopped out of their bodies and into the world like a placenta. This kind of engagement, if you can call it that, is deeply demeaning. It reads like an avoidance tactic, an implicit admission that the work doesn't deserve serious and sustained critical attention.

And perhaps, sometimes, it doesn't. In an ecosystem that runs on the intimate exposure of pain, it makes sense that style might be lower down the list of priorities. The faulty syllogism of the white female–dominated confessional essay—*my writing is messy because it's vulnerable, the vulnerability of my subject position is inherently radical, and therefore formal messiness is politically necessary*—lingers in the genre's ancestry. Once again, culpability happens at multiple links in the chain. If stories about the pain of being racialized are going at a high market rate, then editors are professionally incentivized to coax that out of the work, stat (even if a writer may be trying to convey something else). If a writer's artistic mandate is to prove that her identity is an endless source of agony, that agenda limits numerous possibilities for storytelling and argument. It also establishes a particular set of aesthetic priorities: Spectacle. Voyeurism. Pain. None of these things are anathema to a fancy prose style but, like Bruce Wayne and his alter ego, you don't often see them at the same bat time.

A laissez-faire approach to form might be prevalent and convenient, but it's never been inherent—it's nurture more than nature. The mold of the confessional was cast in very specific circumstances: Pieces needed tight turnarounds to fill content deficits, so they weren't always subject to the most rigorous edits. Aimed at claiming eyeballs, they partook in a limited, garish palette of affects. Their engagement with social questions may have been more interested in provocation than analysis. They engaged subjects (trauma, intimacy, the body) that were messy by definition, and some seepage between content and form is forgivable. They were frequently authored by emerging writers whose voices hadn't crystallized, their experience corresponding with the pittance outlets could afford to pay them. Somewhere along the line, these situational contingencies got annexed to the form and now they get passed off as intrinsic to the genre. But this is not an accurate reflection of the state of the essay. Nor is it a good enough tool kit to attack an issue the size and significance of contemporary subjectivity.

This approach to writing the self is not the only one, or even the dominant one. It just happens to be the one that fits comfortably into what a white readership expects, which in turn guarantees its extreme visibility. It colonizes the internet when bad things happen, and it looms over the way racialized essayists get read at all. So much deliberate, inventive beauty is ignored in favor of being first to name the *urgent*, the *raw*, the *necessary*. It's far too convenient, given the writers who've managed to ride the personal-essay wave, that as soon as we arrive onshore, we automatically get docked points for style.

NONE OF THIS is meant to be a case against pain. By all means, hurt me; I can handle it. I'll be more into it if you're also a stylish conversationalist who can make me laugh, but trust me, I can take it. I'm an editor. We have an entire lexicon of safe words for this kind of thing.

For as long as there are other people, there will be pain. Pain by itself is too easy, though, and it so often feels inert when left alone on the page. It is an inadequate container for the world, or the news, or the individual mind. As the sole support system for a personal story, suffering can feel like it exists more to serve the reader than the writer—to indulge her curiosity, or take her on a tour through someone else's trauma, or confirm an existential awfulness she may have already suspected was there. The writers willing to play that game should get their money by all means. But it shouldn't be the cost of entry to publication, and it shouldn't be the only set of terms by which writers get to tell the stories of themselves.

Pain *by itself* is too easy. But it's possible to refract it outward as part of a spectrum. Let's be real: Suffering is juicy as hell. History and culture and politics bend through it like light in water. Good writers know this, but they also know what to do with it.

A TV interviewer once asked James Baldwin how it felt to start out as a writer who had to clear the triple hurdle of being Black, poor, and gay—his framing, not mine. "You must have said to yourself," the journalist asked, probably already slavering at the imagined answer, "'Gee, how disadvantaged can I get?'"

"No. I thought I hit the jackpot." Baldwin grinned.

The interviewer had clearly been hoping for something sexier, more agonized. "Oh, great."

"It was so outrageous, you could not go any further," Baldwin continued after the laughter, his own and the studio audience's, had subsided. "You had to find a way to use it."

Some of My Best Friends

The white girls ordered salads from the bagel place. They moved in packs—they'd met at dance and sealed their bonds at camp. They ringed their eyes in liner and whispered all through class in snappy phrases thick with *likes*. They tugged on their own shirts like anxious kids to clear more skin below their Tiffany heart tags. Before they all grew up to wife men just like their fathers, they told their mothers to *shut up* at the dinner table—a crime I witnessed more than once that made me giggle in panic. They modeled yoga pants before I knew what yoga was and racism before I knew what race was. I knew something was obviously up, but I didn't call them *white girls* at the time. I just called them *girls*.

White femininity used to be so much less visible. I bobbed all the way to junior high before I knew I was surrounded by it, like the commencement-speech parable about the fish oblivious to what they swim in. (*This Is White Girl.*) I would imitate their upspeak like a tic, wear the yoga pants for how they slid against my legs, flat-iron my hair for five minutes of bliss before my roots revolted. Yet I sooner could have told you what I wasn't than what they were. This is how white womanhood was once meant to seem—like a substance so pure and universal you don't even realize you're inhaling it.

It was invisible to white women, too. In the early nineties, sociologist Ruth Frankenberg published *White Women, Race Matters*, a study that asked how race shapes white women's lives. The answer, according to her interview subjects, was *not much*. For these women, race erupts in memories of segregated childhoods, or brief encounters with disapproval for romancing across the color line, but otherwise they believed they lived raceless lives. "While none of the women I interviewed felt that they were *not* white," Frankenberg admits, "whiteness seemed to be neither a clearly definable cultural terrain nor, for many of them, a desirable one." For centuries now, feminists of color have worked to define that terrain. Mainstream culture has finally caught up and twigged: white femininity is not an element, but a compound. Now, when a white woman weeps, more people hesitate before offering sympathy. When she calls the cops, Twitter calls her Karen. Now, people say *white girl* like it's a term they've just learned for a changing climate's ominous new weather pattern—*you felt that, too, right? It wasn't just me?*

Their visibility is everywhere—in memes, corporate statements, think pieces, a spate of book-length reappraisals of contemporary and historical feminism. Some of the critiques of white femininity have even started coming from powerful white women themselves. They have stepped into the limelight to check their privilege and promise to listen. They've built antiracism juggernauts to explain white fragility to white people, said sorry for blitzscaling their feminist coworking spaces on the backs of their Black employees, and paid five grand to have racialized women pick apart their biases at dinner parties until they cry. But these apologies, if that's what they are, haven't diminished white women's ability to accrue power, whether those accolades take shape as capital or praise. Many of these gestures blur the line between contrition for past wrongs and the expectation that they'll be rewarded for admitting them.

White femininity is very, enviably good at this—metabolizing critique and converting it into a moral, political, or financial asset.

It's a move that gets repeated all over popular culture. Here's a partial inventory of things white femininity has celebrated or reclaimed:

- having friends
- having feelings
- not having feelings
- being ambitious
- being sad
- being messy
- being difficult
- caring too much
- not caring at all
- turning any of this into art

Of course, these are things that everybody does. But it's mostly white women who get to be their canonized ambassadors. The list isn't an exhaustive taxonomy, but it captures a number of the major female-driven cultural shifts of the last several decades—the '90s trauma memoir, the rom-com peak, confessional songwriting, girlboss feminism, the true-crime mania, the personal-essay explosion—all genres whose whiteness has been well-documented. There's power, to be sure, in reclaiming these traits. Before they became artistic principles or cause for celebration, many of them began as gendered insults. To take back these so-called weaknesses is a tiny correction in the ongoing assault on the autonomy and self-expression of anyone who's not a cisgender male. It's good and necessary work. But too often, these same sites of feminine assertion become contested territory.

White women are marginalized by virtue of their gender but insulated by racial privilege. This is an obvious point, but it also presents an awkward tension to navigate. In answer to it, white women have evolved a number of tactics to maintain a position as ones who both have and have not. Crying when threatened is a popular one. So is casting oneself as an outsider despite all evidence to the contrary: "I think feminism has a hard time being inclusive of a lot of things that I am," *Untamed* memoirist and activist Glennon Doyle told *The New Yorker*. Doyle was specifically talking about her "femme presentation" and her "high-pitched voice," which aren't exactly markers of radical otherness. More to the point, though, Doyle is also a thin, conventionally attractive white woman with a net worth in the millions (literally all the things feminism has a very easy time being inclusive of). The third-wave feminist maxim, *the personal is political*, has also become an overloaded catchall for the political weight of private traumas. These strategies are everywhere: They have birthed entire cultural movements, they masquerade as what popularly gets called feminism, they shape conversations and transactions between white and racialized women. We have learned to clock most of these infelicities when they appear. But others still pass unnoticed. If we counted every tactic by which white femininity patrols its borders and reverse-engineered them into a map, we might get something like this:

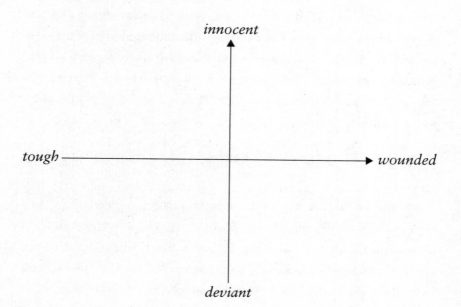

These are the cardinal directions. Entire pockets of culture have sprung up at each point of the compass: extensive theorizations of female pain, catalogues of women's sharp intellectual achievements, proof of their goodness, and paeans to their deviance. My aim is not to grade white women along any particular scale—I love white women; they are, truly, some of my best friends—but to think about how the borders of white femininity get defended and which bodies get expelled in the name of self-protection or even progress.

SADNESS WAS THE first tentacle to reach me, reel me in, and make me think that I could do it, too. I was writing songs at fourteen when a friend pointed me, fatefully, toward Fiona Apple and Tori Amos. The piano, my lifelong instrument, does sorrow far better than it does cheer, and I'd already rejected joy for being boring. But I also felt that the tools I had to work with—basic minor chords and objectless teenage melancholy—were insufficient to express the size and depth of what it was I really felt.

Hearing Apple and Amos was like accessing a different plane. Huge, difficult things had happened to them both—sexual violence, mental illness, the breakdown of serious relationships. I was transfixed and turned on and concerned by their suffering, the size and severity of it. These women weren't just *sad*. They were *wounded*. Their wounds gave way to sonic landscapes with textures I'd never encountered, in music or otherwise. I heard things done to a piano I didn't know you were allowed to do to a piano. Curled up on the floor in front of my CD player and listening to *Tidal* for the first time, I felt the sinking certainty that I'd never be that good. There was already a ceiling on whatever I'd achieve because someone else had written the surprising, inevitable, world-ending piano riff for "Never Is a Promise" before I'd even thought to go looking for it. You can't recover from a deficit like that. But there was also, I realized, a lesson here, about how you mediate your pain for your art. I had never let myself linger in my melancholy the way these women did, luxuriating in it till my skin turned pruny. I'd been dressing up my sads, giving them little hats like elaborate piano runs and wordy turns of phrase. Now, I realized, I could just strip down and wallow.

You can draw a clean line in the before and the after of my songwriting. I wrote and sang about the same things I had before— imagined or abortive teenage relationships, minor personal slights, deep dives into moments from Neil Gaiman novels that had moved me. But the form of my songs cracked open and began to sprawl. Pieces stretched to twice their old length, with enigmatic titles that might appear once in the lyrics but never got repeated in the chorus. My tidy chords bloated into sevenths and ninths and elevenths. With more room in which to feel things, the quality of that feeling also changed. I dwelled and ruminated. Discovered there were things to be sad about I hadn't even known were worth my tears. I understood that what I'd been doing before was purely dabbling. This, however, was art.

The music industry did not want me to be sad the way these women were. When I felt confident enough to meet with performance coaches and other industry professionals, I heard this message very clearly. They did not vibe with my signature look—a blazer over jeans and various Hot Topic T-shirts, a pair of striped fingerless gloves that I thought looked daring on the keys (and which my partner finally convinced me to throw out, like, last year). *Why are you always behind the piano?* the people I met with asked me. *Why don't you wear your hair bigger? Have you considered backup dancers? Have you ever seen* Prince's *backup dancers?* To look at me in my ripped jeans and Green Day T-shirts was to see very clearly that none of what they described—the hair, the backup dancers, any of it—was anywhere near what I was going for, aesthetically. But that didn't stop them. One man, in a meeting with me and my dad, told me to go home and light some candles, get high, and think about how I could start acting sexier onstage. Part of this is just the rank commercialism of all creative industries, people trying to steer you toward whatever will turn the biggest profit. But the other part was that they saw biracial Black girl plus piano and landed on the unimaginative sum of "Alicia Keys." It was not my place to make people cry, or even to cry myself. I was supposed to make them *groove*.

So, not everyone gets to be sad. But elsewhere, the closed circuit between having feelings and making art has been allowed to thrive. In the essay "Grand Unified Theory of Female Pain," Leslie Jamison aims to unpick the seam between creativity and suffering. The piece taxonomizes all the ways in which (white) women can hurt, from Sylvia Plath to Lena Dunham, from Miss Havisham to Jamison herself, and grapples with our questionable impulse to glamorize it. Though Jamison is critical of how culture has "turned the wounded woman into a kind of goddess" when theorizing pain, she also can't resist romanticizing her own. Worrying the wound is inherently pleasurable but, even better, it can become a whole personality and artistic practice: "Wounds promise authenticity and profundity," Jamison sighs. "Beauty and singularity, desirability . . . They bleed enough light to write by." This is the same thing I intuited while listening to Fiona Apple and Tori Amos and various other white female balladeers. It hurts too good to stop, but more importantly, if you're always in pain you'll never want for material.

This principle transcends the music genre. In white female–authored projects, luxuriant woundedness is everywhere. To be born is to be wounded: After her resigned expulsion from the womb, Melissa Broder laments in the essay collection *So Sad Today*, "they probably put me in a room with, like, twenty other babies. Immediately, I'm sure I compared myself to all of them and lost." As a child, she eats her fingernails, earwax, snot, and vaginal secretions to contend with the pain of being alive. Aging does not mitigate the suffering:

"Single older women, as a demographic, are as fucked a group as can ever exist," Zoe (Frances McDormand), a women's studies professor, tells the turtlenecked Erica (Diane Keaton). The two of them, a pair of sisters in Nancy Meyers's *Something's Gotta Give*, are having a little confab about oppression as they wash dishes in the kitchen of Erica's Hamptons mansion. (Later, when she's spurned both of her suitors—Keanu Reeves and Jack Nicholson—Keaton spends four back-to-back scenes spewing what the script calls "the kind of tears that have been thirty years in the making," a hallmark of the Meyers-verse.)

The existential agony can be particularly acute in adolescence and early adulthood, when all the feels of teen girlhood hit the thankless wall of reality. In an episode of *Girls*, Hannah Horvath and Marnie Michaels (played by writer-director Lena Dunham and Allison Williams) screech back and forth across their Brooklyn apartment, with a kind of meta-glee, about which one of them is really and truly "a big, ugly wound." The wound is also the wellspring of creation; in the words of Nora Ephron, herself no stranger to pain, "Everything is copy." The point of the Nancy Meyers montage isn't just that Diane Keaton's continuous weeping is meant to be funny, but that the waterworks are taking place while her character is, as the script says, "writing at a breakneck pace." Gushing from the wound is a tidal wave of creative juice. Why would you want to plug that up? Without your hurt, what even are you? If you're Hannah Horvath, you don't even exist!

These aren't just expressions of standard-issue suffering—it's life, of course it fucking hurts—they're also tiny contests that assert how unique their creators are by virtue of the wound: I was born *the most* dysfunctional baby. I am a member of *the most* oppressed group to ever live. I am *so* attractive and successful that feminism doesn't even want me. I have *all* the feelings. I *am* the wound. At least some of this narcissism tries to be self-aware—Dunham knows how awful Hannah is, Broder's always angling for the punch line—and these works have deserved both the praise and criticism they've received in response to their self-involvement. But what is it that's making these women hurt so badly? With their Brooklyn apartments and their Hamptons mansions, you'd think they have it pretty good. Why are they so committed to standing their ground on not just the intensity of their pain, but the singularity of it?

It comes back to the line white women walk between privilege and disadvantage. Because whiteness is often assumed to be the mouthpiece of "universal" storytelling, white women are freed from the expectation that their work engage with politics or represent a marginalized group. Accordingly, they can be as niche and inward-looking in their art as they please. Their work can exist in an imagined universe devoid of racialized people—it almost *has* to in order for its internal logic to hold; as people have observed of *Girls* and Nancy Meyers's films, it often does. Meyers's claim to the paramount suffering of older single white females would have scanned very differently if there'd been a Black woman present. In a world composed exclusively of white men and white women, it's true, older single women probably *would* be as fucked a group as could ever exist. An essay on the "Grand Unified Theory of *Black* Female Pain," one assumes, would aestheticize bodies very differently and be far less romantic about the histories of violence done to them. But many of these creators, having flushed the less convenient forms of marginality from their presence, then exaggerate their own weakness as evidence of their work's political gravity.

Of course, feminine expression *is* politicized—women's speech and agency have always been a target for misogyny. Ditto our pain. Men have been hurling agony at us like a curse from time—*In pain you shall bring forth children*—and then refusing to believe in that pain's severity or existence. But add white privilege to the mix and, all too often, watch as the link between personal and political stretches like taffy. The maxim that *the personal is political* can parry virtually any criticism, no matter how deserved, that gets thrust at the art of feminine confession. A text can shrink down to the stone of the individual, an ouroboros of pain concerned with nothing beyond its own endless chomp and, however gently you suggest its creator might look outside herself a bit more, she can snap back that her sorrow is actually radical. It must be really nice to create something, especially something steeped in pain and tears, without worrying someone will say it's *about identity*. But maybe the deeper fear is that no one will. That abject word can still seem to confer such delicious urgency.

Like having friends or feelings, these approaches to artistry are not embodied by every white non-male artist. Nor are they unique to them. My earliest fiction didn't have many Black people in it, either. But extreme vulnerability has hardened into an example of white femininity because it's been curated to be exactly that. Feminine sadness has sealed itself up and pushed out other participants. Safy-Hallan Farah documents this process in "All Alone in Their White Girl Pain," an essay on the segregated online life of "Sad Girl Theory." Farah looks at figures like Lana Del Rey and Audrey Wollen, women who aestheticize their agony and call it politically subversive. The reason "White Sad Girl" took the form she did is not because only white girls are sad, or that all teen girls on Tumblr are white. The sad white girls symbolize what Farah calls "the first America," a national fantasy that ignores the many "other Americas"—the browner ones, the poorer ones—while celebrating its own stainless virtue. Of course, it's not only white girls who were ever sad, or objectified online, or called vulnerable. But you wouldn't know that from how the digital trend took shape.

Audrey Wollen was part of the constellation of artists and texts—including Broder, Lana Del Rey, the "Teen-Girl Tumblr Aesthetic," and *Rookie* magazine—which were keen to express a distinct digital despair. Wollen would take photos of herself in states of vulnerability, lying in a field or crying in the mirror, and post them on Instagram alongside the language of protest. This was what she called "Sad Girl Theory": "Political protest," she told *Dazed*, "is usually defined in [the] masculine terms" of march, riot, or occupation. "But I think that this limited spectrum of activism excludes a whole history of girls who have used their sorrow and their self-destruction to disrupt systems of domination." This limited spectrum of activism has also gotten a lot of shit done. Wollen spins entire histories of liberatory struggles into a gendered insult, and casts her response—which, again, is pictures of herself crying—as commensurate with these collective movements. There is nothing inherently wrong with crying, or photographing it while crouched in a sink. Nor is it a sin to skip the uprising. It can be physically impossible, by dint of ability, for someone to put their body in the streets, and there are many other ways to show solidarity. But where it gets weird is when those acts of sitting out become evidence of ethical and political superiority.

This isn't new; the Romantics had a thing for fetishizing sadness and invalidism, too. For them, being sorrowful or sick were also pathways to a rarified specialness. As Susan Sontag writes in *Illness as Metaphor*, "The melancholy character—or the tubercular—was a superior one: sensitive, creative, a being apart." Being ill in body or spirit buffed one's sensibility and, by extension, one's artistic output; "Sadness," Sontag deadpans, "made one 'interesting.'" White women rely on a similar trade-off when they market the art of suffering as being politically engaged. With no social commitments beyond the personal, they're forced to inflate the stock on their own vulnerability, asserting not just its inherent value but its capacity, as Wollen says, as "a gesture of liberation." But liberation for whom? The only way to retain this death grip on sadness is by comparison; by performing it as an excess that surpasses, even erases, other kinds of marginality. Keep calling racialized artists *gritty* and you can stand your ground on *radical softness*. I am a member of *the most* oppressed group to ever live. I am *so* attractive and successful that feminism doesn't even want me. I have *all* the feelings. I *am* the wound.

SUFFERING, AS A strategy, can only get you so far. In the face of new political attacks, like the ones promised and delivered on by the 2016 election, many groups of people—not just women—needed to build a new vocabulary. Vulnerability might seem to have a sexy political valence, but when your rights are under assault, it can also be a liability. A number of cultural and political events, some of them related to the election, clustered around this moment: #MeToo ignited, *Girls* ended, women marched, Ferrante Fever spiked, *The Handmaid's Tale* TV series started, the personal-essay crested, Elizabeth Warren persisted. Messy self-exposure suddenly seemed like the relic of another era. This was an age of hardened shells. A different kind of woman became the icon that the time demanded.

On the cover of Michelle Dean's group biography, *Sharp: The Women Who Made an Art of Having an Opinion*, illustrations of six of her subjects render them eminently well-dressed. In the words of Joan Didion, one of the book's cover stars, "style is character." This is a truism of both their prose and their persons: Renata Adler's silver braid draped over a jacketed shoulder, Nora Ephron's tiny bangs and turtleneck, Didion's blunt bob and all-black fit. In their writing, many of these women tackle weighty subjects—totalitarianism, law, illness, death—which often happen to be ones in which they have a personal stake. But that *personal* is never rendered in tones that are especially emotional, which is a point of pride among their admirers. After the 2016 election, figures like Didion, Sontag, Hannah Arendt, Simone Weil, Rebecca West, and Mary McCarthy caught a second wind. Though these writers were very much public intellectuals in their own time, their work attracted new attention as America fast-tracked toward tragedy. It used to be that Didion's face wasn't even on her own book covers. Now, it's on billboards and tote bags.

Dean's *Sharp* was published in 2018, the year after Deborah Nelson's *Tough Enough: Arbus, Arendt, Didion, McCarthy, Sontag, Weil*. The two books focused on overlapping Venn diagrams of female intellectuals; Dean's, a wider circle, encompasses West, Arendt, McCarthy, Sontag, Didion, Adler, Ephron, Dorothy Parker, Pauline Kael, Janet Malcolm, Lillian Hellman, and Zora Neale Hurston (thrown against a sharp white background). Both projects arise from a similar impulse, gathering their biographical subjects under an adjective that was used, at one time or another, to describe each of them. Both authors seek to reclaim a coded, gendered insult—not unlike how the art of woundedness snatched back terms like *sad girl* and *too much*. These women, Dean writes, "came up in a world that was not eager to hear women's opinions about anything." They were also little proto–girl bosses, lacking the benefit—sometimes because of their own antipathy toward the idea—of an organized feminist movement. (Perhaps they also thought feminism would have a hard time being inclusive of the things they were.) But, unlike the women who made an art of having feelings or a body, their turf was eked out and defended by the mind alone. It was by virtue of "their exceptional talent [that] they were granted a kind of intellectual equality to men other women had no hope of," which, as far as meritocracies go, is a very grim one.

Unsurprisingly, men gave them shit for it. More often than celebrating their sharpness, Dean writes, "people reacted badly to the sting." Nelson's subjects attracted labels like *cold* and *clinical* and *pitiless* and *heartless*, all unimaginative code words for *bad woman*. But this same toughness enables them to prioritize "the object of reflection over feelings about that object"—a cardinal virtue in a critic. Their precision of thought gives way to a moral clarity, one that lends itself to actionable forms of empathy, even if it didn't always translate into feminist solidarity or conventionally gendered shows of senti-ment. These women weren't staging their own agony; they were re-garding the pain of others. By toning down emotionality, they could bear witness more reliably, "looking at painful reality with directness and clarity and without consolation or compensation." They were, in every sense of the word, *cool*.

Of course, there were other intellectuals who could've been can-onized for their coolness, their moral clarity. In my own essays, I longed to be cold and clinical and pitiless in a way that challenged men on their intellectual ground and granted me parity with them. But I wasn't supposed to write about that. I was supposed to write about how hard it was to be alive in a body like mine. Like indulg-ing in unbridled sadness, to be able to cut emotion out of your work wholesale is its own form of privilege. Reviews of both Dean's and Nelson's books have cited the whiteness of their subject groups. Dean herself addresses this in her book's introduction, noting that all of the women come from similar backgrounds—white, middle-class, and mostly Jewish—apart from Zora Neale Hurston, whom she includes as a correction to a clique that excluded her. But Dean's minor modification ends up throwing the problem into greater relief—the link between whiteness and being thought of as intellec-tually *sharp* or *tough* isn't really examined at length. That link comes back to white femininity's vexed relationship with marginalization. It's comparatively easy for white women to strip away their own body politics to speak as a vessel of pure intellect. A white woman writing about camp or totalitarianism or the law can be considered universal. A Black woman doing ethnographic work, or writing about a Black woman on trial—both of which Hurston did—is more commonly considered niche, special interest. Only the former gets to be that prized commodity: relatable.

We rarely use the word *relatable* uncritically anymore, at least without a suffix like *to whom*, but we do still use it—especially as praise for seeming to express something that feels true. But *relatable*, while pretending to let the whole world in, actually shuts out more than it opens up. Relatability calls upon "the language of personal preference to legitimize the narrowness and rigidity of the collective white imagination," writes Rafia Zakaria in *Against White Feminism*. To gain entry into white and middle-class halls of power, it helps if you speak the language. White-dominated fields, like NGOs or newsrooms (two of Zakaria's examples), normalize the kinds of lived experiences they like to see beamed back at them. Similarly, they prefer discreet silence on things they like to believe *don't* apply to white life, like "certain kinds of migration" or "certain kinds of internecine conflict." *Relatable* is Diane Keaton weeping in her Hamptons kitchen about how awful men are. *Relatable* is not weeping in your studio apartment kitchen over how awful racism is. *Relatable* is Nora Ephron feeling bad about her neck. It is not feeling bad about every other part of yourself because of the accretive exhaustion of systems made to break bodies like yours. *Relatable* is what Ellen DeGeneres called her 2018 Netflix stand-up special, two years before the backlash against her. *Relatable* is the least amount of work required to achieve a perfect overlay between yourself and the world, a hall of mirrors that's constantly reflecting back to you exactly what it is you want to see, which is simply yourself. Sad white women looking at other sad white women looking at themselves in the mirror.

Recently, I picked up my first book by Nora Ephron—one of the women included in Michelle Dean's group—on the advice of someone I trust. I was trying, fittingly, to think through how one might become more relatable on the page, and Ephron's name kept coming up. I knew Ephron's films but had never read her work, so I decided to try it out. A few short essays into *I Feel Bad About My Neck*, I was staggered by the lengths this woman goes to in order to make out that she's just one of us. Sure, she feels bad about lowest-common-denominator things like her neck and her body hair and her bad eyesight and how much it sucks to carry a handbag. Okay. I can relate, sort of. But I didn't realize coming for "Oh no, my turkey wattle" meant staying for "I make upwards of $250,000, and it's a tragedy they want to raise my property taxes." This was in 1980. Incredibly, the space and time she devotes to bemoaning luxury real estate—that she can afford on an astonishing salary even before you factor in inflation!!!—has not left a tiny ding in the way people talk about her. That she gets cited for being relatable speaks to her skill and the warmth of her voice, certainly. But it also indicates the considerable amount of latitude people are willing to give her when they read her work.

I sometimes have trouble connecting with the work of sharp, tough women. I think it's because I first encountered them through their contemporary imitators, who all but ruined them for me. I was never moved to fetishize women for being unsentimental; that, too, felt like as big a grift as vulnerability sometimes did. White women already won the campaign to monopolize feeling—now they wanted to have *unfeeling*, too? In criticism now, it can sometimes feel like flintiness gets fetishized to excess, then called feminist. A brutal review that veers into personal attack is a permissible flex because it's hip to be glib. I'm not coming out against tough criticism or bad reviews—there's nothing like a perfect pan. Moreover, these days our best literary critics aren't white women at all. I'm thinking more about the cranky, overly broad takes like *YA sucks* and *why are we still reading personal essays?* and *all contemporary fiction panders to us like we're children*, all of which I've seen in the past two years. Such critics do not think unfiltered emoting is a win for the gender; in fact, they've probably given the books that do it bad reviews.

Part of me wants to sympathize with the glib young literary woman. I also have high aesthetic standards and I love to read good criticism. But as an antidote to vulnerability, this feels like trading one set of affects for another. Saying feelings are dumb doesn't seem much more interesting than wallowing in them. Both poses are disengaged from the collective, whether out of narcissistic self-absorption or because you're too busy shouting that you're not like those other girls.

WITH GREATER VISIBILITY comes increased scrutiny. If you want to prove your pure intentions, the bar is higher than it used to be. "My entire moral code, as a kid and now, is a need to be thought of as *good*." That's Taylor Swift tipping her hand in *Miss Americana*, the Netflix documentary about her life and career. The line isn't specifically about Swift's politics; it's more a general principle of her self-esteem. Reflecting on the fallout when Kanye West grabbed the mic from her at the 2009 Video Music Awards, Swift admits that when she thought she heard the crowd booing at her, it was especially traumatic as "someone who's built their whole belief system on getting people to clap for [her]." But elsewhere in the doc, when she breaks her years-long political silence to speak out against a Republican Tennessee senator, her reasoning sounds more or less the same. "I need to be on the right side of history," she says, on the decision to finally get political. The choice is so agonized partly because we put pressure on celebrities to speak on political causes, and partly because their earning potential depends on their strategic advocacy or silence. Swift has probably been hearing "don't be the Dixie Chicks" her whole career. But, as far as moral codes go, she plays it pretty safe. Wanting to be *thought of* as good, after all, is not the same as wanting to *be* good, full stop.

That doesn't mean people can't tell the difference. Look what happened to Ellen DeGeneres, queen of relatability, whose empire operated under the motto "Be Kind." Despite this dedicated branding, BuzzFeed reported that many employees working on *The Ellen Show* had a different experience. Current and former staffers described incidents of workplace racism, harassment, and toxicity. None of the critiques were of DeGeneres herself (though there were other allegations about her temperament circulating on social media around the same time), but they were about the environment she'd let fester while selling merch that said "Be Kind to One Another." A year later, when DeGeneres announced that her beloved show would end after its nineteenth season, she addressed the criticisms. She called them "misogynistic" and compared them to the backlash she faced when she first came out as a lesbian in the 1990s.

This was a deeply cynical response, and people saw it for what it was. DeGeneres's reply framed the critiques of her workplace as a personal attack—one that invoked, at least tangentially, the way she'd been discriminated against in the past. While the allegations were about abuses of power, her response emphasized her powerless-ness. All things considered, this was a fairly decent attempt to try to save a sinking ship. If you peek into the white-fragility tool kit, history suggests this sort of thing usually works. Except—and here's where she went wrong—these moves don't work the same way any-more. They've gotten too recognizable. The public has learned to call bullshit. Now, when white women try to weaponize their tears to prove how they've been wronged, they're more likely to become the subjects of grainy cell phone videos. They get quirky, alliterative viral nicknames that testify to their sin.

In *White Tears, Brown Scars*, Ruby Hamad traces the roots of turn-ing on the waterworks. White women, Hamad writes, have the whole weight of history behind them, an entire apparatus of pro-tecting female virtue through violent white supremacy. All she needs to do is tear up and they'll send in the troops, and she knows it. If feminism's third wave belabored that the personal was political, then the fourth wave reverses those terms: what Hamad calls "Strategic White Womanhood . . . makes personal what is political." You think I'm fostering a toxic workplace? Well, *you* must just hate me because

I'm a *woman*. Hamad documents a string of interactions in which an attempt at conversation—usually between a white woman and a racialized woman, and usually about a politicized issue—gets derailed when the white woman feels attacked and starts crying. Strategic white womanhood is "a spectacle that permits the actual issue at hand to take a back seat to the emotions of the white woman." This isn't powerlessness, Hamad points out; it's power that pretends to be powerless.

Nowadays, we expect people will be more self-aware about holding power and quicker to admit how they benefit from it. But what do you do if you know power is icky but you worked hard to get it and really want to keep it? To smooth out such dissonance, we now have the very modern genre of the privilege disclaimer. In *White Feminism*, Koa Beck figures these cursory privilege checks as "the cul-de-sac of white feminism—the way by which you go through the motions of racial or queer consciousness, but actually just come out the same way you went in." Privilege disclaimers are like magic tricks. They can turn complex, awkward material realities—generational wealth, whiteness, the ability to pass within a certain social category—into words, dispensed with as easily as breath. Of course, there is value in explaining the ways we're both sidelined by and complicit in structures of power. It's a tool for building solidarity and a step toward liberation. But that's not the way the tool often gets used now, which is closer to a waiver you sign before you go skydiving. Any risk of criticism you might attract for your privilege, no matter how deserved, can be preempted by simply copping to it first. "I surprised my closest inner circle with a trip to a private island," Kim Kardashian West infamously posted on social media, a trip that "humbly reminded" her "of how privileged her life is." *You can't criticize me for my power,* the logic goes, *because I admitted to it already.* A privilege disclaimer acts as a kind of insulation. Within its shelter, the speaker can feel excused from having to reckon with questions like, say, whether the existence of billionaires is immoral. By that calculus, she can still think of herself as blameless rather than complicit.

But, again, the bar is higher than it used to be. The rhetoric of social justice circulates more easily than ever. Its meaning may degrade with bad usage, but it's increasingly available to tap into as a business strategy. You can build a women's-only coworking space with brutal efficiency because it stands for the cause of gender equality. You can speak out against a racist, homophobic senator and know that this will keep you firmly on the right side of both history and profit. You can build, as Robin DiAngelo has, a whole empire on white guilt. DiAngelo, a DEI consultant, is the author of the bestselling *White Fragility* and *Nice Racism*. *Nice Racism*, the more recent book, contends that the "niceness" of white progressives causes more daily harm to racialized people than they realize (and, in the aggregate, than violent white supremacists do, as violent white supremacists aren't something racialized people necessarily encounter as often). Her own whiteness, she tells *The New Yorker*, gives her "an insider's perspective" that makes white people more likely to listen to her than they would a person of color "point[ing] the finger." Whiteness, in DiAngelo's view, is both qualification and permission. Sad white people looking at other sad white people looking at themselves in the mirror.

To be good, to truly *be* good and not just *seem* good, means letting go of power. For some people, that prospect is terrifying enough to drop the pretense of even trying. Lana Del Rey, one of the leading faces of Sad Girl Theory, let the mask drop with her viral "Question for the culture" Instagram post. In the post, Del Rey calls out a list of Black, racialized, and racially ambiguous female artists— all of whose stars have risen higher than hers—whom she sees her own music as having "paved the way for." Lana laments that women like Beyoncé and Cardi B and Doja Cat and Ariana Grande get a free pass for "songs about being sexy, wearing no clothes, fucking, cheating, etc." while Lana herself gets "crucified" for "glamorizing abuse." The hurt here is double-glazed: the anxiety of influence for which she gets no credit, and her own segregation when she felt she ought to have been canonized.

Del Rey concludes, against the weight of all of history and culture, that there is no "place in feminism for women who look and act like me." This move should be familiar by now; a way to hold on to the sexiness of weakness in a world unsexily designed for your supremacy. Her claim to victimhood reads like an anti-privilege check, a fragment of a bygone world. Almost a year later, following a pan-industry crisis over anti-Black racism in which she might have taken a beat to reflect, she released the cover of her next album—a group of women from visibly varied ethnic and racial backgrounds—and pointed to her friends of color as evidence for how she has "always been extremely inclusive without even trying to." The public insisted on making it a "WOC/POC issue" when the truth of it, Del Rey explained, was that "[her] best friends are rappers."

THE BRANDING EXERCISE of contemporary feminism means that almost any act—of vulnerability, toughness, capitalism, coveting the power men have and wielding it the way men do—can be lauded as inherently political. Like reading Nora Ephron as relatable, this gives white women a high level of latitude. She doesn't even have to waste time being good—she can get away with whatever she wants and we'll canonize her just the same. Does anybody care if Susan Sontag was an especially *good* person? The absence of virtuousness might even be what makes a given character appealing in the first place. Difficulty, too, has been claimed as a form of empowerment.

Whether she's flouting normative beauty standards or the laws against homicide, the difficult woman is a popular candidate for a protagonist and an object of pop-culture fetish. She boils bunnies, joins cults, totes guns out on her lawn. In real life, she's likely to be a source of horror, though that horror often gives way to eventual fascination. Privilege insulates her from the harshest consequences of her actions, but she'll never feel compelled to cop to it. Fiction loves these difficult women, the gone girls and the grifters and the outsiders too wild to obey the same scripts as the rest of us. She's always opting out of stifling social contracts, like the narrator of Ottessa Moshfegh's novel *My Year of Rest and Relaxation*, whose ability to enter a yearlong drug coma is made possible by her wealth and whiteness. On some level, this protagonist is a release valve. Women in stories and out of them have spent so long laboring under the directive to be *likable*, there's still a special charge in departing from it.

White women are allowed a similar freedom in nonfiction, glorifying in the palette of stories they're allowed to tell. The first essay in Melissa Broder's *So Sad Today*, where she talks about consuming her own fluids, culminates in a dream of "devour[ing] herself whole," a child allowed to "eat the shit out of herself and then shit herself out." Historically, white women have had more permission in their personal writing to describe things like their bodily emissions and sex lives and drug use. But they're also exempt from the *pressure* to sensationalize their lives the way racialized writers are, and they're not expected to describe the burdens of living in a certain body (though they often still choose to). This woman is a warning that the lives of girls and women are a pressure-cooker, but she is also an object lesson in what some people get away with when they boil over.

If and when she does, whether in the pages of a memoir or out on the street, she can still become an object of enchantment. Culture is still learning how to sift the revolutionary from the reactionary when it comes to female rage, which is one possible explanation for why "white women voted for Trump" has passed into a kind of weird mantra, a refrain both knowing and perplexed. Sometimes an expression of fury is patently bad, an exercise in unbridled entitlement. The spectacle of Karen-spotting reached a new level with Patricia McCloskey, who stood alongside her husband on their St. Louis property and was photographed brandishing a gun at nearby protesters. More viscerally than other viral white women, McCloskey embodied the violence of the scene; the latent nightmare white rage always runs the risk of becoming. At other times, feminine anger retains a trace amount of innocence that can make it hard to interpret. In an essay for *The Baffler*, published when the summer of McCloskey and Amy Cooper had just ended, Niela Orr unpacks the enduring fascination with white feminine lethality. Orr tracks the murderous woman as she unfurls across various forms; how, in a list of genres including true crime and docudrama and soap opera and reality TV, "We watch her kill and kill again, always with the same sense of her strangeness," as if every time feels like the first and we can't recognize the pattern. (The pattern is she's always white, conventionally attractive, well-to-do—you know, all those things feminism has a hard time being inclusive of.)

North American viewers are obsessed with this woman, especially when she's based on a true story. We interpret her pain according to a framework so familiar she becomes sympathetic. Orr traces this sympathy through several decades of films, TV adaptations, and cultural trends. Recent examples include white women's "backlash to the 'Karen' nickname" and the popularity and memeification of Carole Baskin (one of the many bombastic personas at the center of the Netflix docuseries *Tiger King*). Both phenomena, Orr argues, are part of an ongoing assertion: There's something fascinating and singular about the "unhinged white woman." She could never be a trope, or a type. She is always an anomaly who deserves at least our attention, if not our admiration.

Fiction inevitably comes back around to scoop these women up. Now they're making a movie called *Karen*, starring Taryn Manning as the histrionically racist neighbor who's literally called Karen. Kate McKinnon is slated to play Carole Baskin in one of the many adaptations of *Tiger King*. Over and over, creators across forms return to the poor little white girls who fell in with Charles Manson. These girls keep receiving complex and compassionate inner lives in fiction, as if their bodies hold the secret of the feminine mystique. This protection of white female deviance is like a covered wagon that shuttles it from innocence to violence and back around to sympathy. Just as we've begun to develop a language for naming what's toxic in white femininity, someone slides in with the qualification *not all Karens*. Maybe this time what she did was romantic, or political, or at least merits further study. No doubt the *Karen* movie will have lines so self-aware, our eyes will skitter in vicarious shame, but the impulse to make the film at all betrays a lack of awareness about what the term *Karen* even does. It's hard not to see this selective fact-finding as that same impulse that takes critique and turns it into profit or cachet. The conversion into story, even a bad story, is the final coronation.

And you know what? This is awkward, but I love a lot of those stories. I eat them up like everyone else. I love their perfect synthesis of virtue and vulnerability; the chaotic cocktail of white women acting tough and having big feelings about it and seeming good while often hiding truly shady shit. The zones of white-girl culture too often feel siloed. We analyze a white woman's tears when they're patently empty but not when she's doing her best to mean it; we criticize her virtuousness as hypocritical when she clearly doesn't care about justice but we also let her get away with murder. White femininity isn't as invisible as it used to be, but its gaps give a lot of freedom to women who still have things to get away with.

But watching it on-screen is pure, anesthetic pleasure. Some cultural critics have called this genre "white mess," a term coined by Crooked Media's *Keep It* podcast to describe what's essentially just "white women with legal problems." Issa Rae invoked the term to profess her love for HBO's *The Undoing*, starring Hugh Grant and Nicole Kidman (a frequent leading lady of the genre, along with her *Big Little Lies* screen-sister Reese Witherspoon). *The Good Wife* is another star of the form; so too is HBO's *The White Lotus* and—a little tangentially but still, I'd argue, part of the family—Netflix's *You*. White mess, journalist Ash Sarkar writes for *Novara Media*, has a distinctive set of trappings: prestige actors, "infidelity, claustrophobic parent-child relationships, a social milieu where everyone nurtures a secret, stunning interiors, murder, white people, cashmere and the best defense lawyer that money can buy." The world of white mess is so hermetic its logic is closer to fantasy. "Wealth is like gravity," Sarkar writes; "it comes from nowhere and is everywhere." If the women happen to work, their hours are uniquely flexible. There is usually at least one racialized person inserted into the scene for a gesture at veracity. The same character usually also acts as a class foil, belonging to the one family that doesn't inhabit a stratospheric income bracket and reminding us—if not the show's characters— that there's a real world that we're willfully averting our eyes from.

But we're not in it for veracity—we're in it to escape. I love to sink into a text in which the worst that can happen is a philandering husband that drained the investment fund earmarked for the foyer renovation, or a minor family emergency that interrupts the job where the protagonist works occasional half days and bills $800 an hour. A glass of cabernet will never taste as good as it looks when Alicia Florrick, swaddled in cashmere, cups it in her pale, bony hands.

Barely Legal

Going to law school was supposed to fix a lot of things. I wanted it to make me sharp and smart and hard. I wanted to be of use, to serve a broader social purpose. I wanted to throw down the gauntlet when people asked me what I did for a living. I wanted to ward off the mess my future might be if I picked a less stable career path. I wanted order, in my life as in the court. Most of all, though, I wanted to know how to turn word into action. Legal reasoning seemed like the purest thing one could ever hope to do with language, like there would never be any dead air or wasted feeling. Law was like poetry, except it could make something happen. If I made a good argument in real life, all I'd get was the satisfaction of being right. But if I made a good argument in the courtroom, I might change the course of history.

These are the fantasies of someone who's watched a lot of legal dramas and conceptualized adulthood as a kind of mood board, but never talked to a working lawyer or tried to read an actual case. Three years of law school and six figures in tuition later, I'd learn that the supposed purity of language is one of the law's biggest grifts. Legal reasoning is not a flawless piece of craftsmanship. (Remember the *Bakke* decision? That thing was full of holes!) Statutes and cases speak the language of fairness and neutrality; for evidence of how that works in practice, look at the state of our social order.

I'm generalizing, here—not all laws—but I'm also describing one of the system's very basic tools. Billion-dollar sectors, like the prison industry, exist in the gaps between the letter of the law and the way it gets applied.

The thing I did get right about the law, though, was its impatience with how messy life was. Legal reasoning brooks no argument with lived complexity. Instead, it prunes away much of the facts and context of a case until only the bare essentials remain. You *can* divine this principle from watching legal dramas, at least crudely, because it's exactly what working in the law does to the characters' lives. Long days at the office end with brief sleeps in big, empty houses full of dark wood furniture and a dope wine cellar, the tomblike silence occasionally broken by the soft upstairs creaks of a resentful spouse. I was also primed to recognize this pattern because it's what I hoped the law would do to me. I was soothed by shows where people walk-and-talked and worked too much, filling every moment in which they might otherwise wonder whether their lives had meaning. To me, the greatest love story in *The West Wing* didn't take place between C.J. Cregg and Toby Ziegler, but C.J. and her job. When she ascends to White House chief of staff, the way Alison Janney delivered the line "You think I'm not aware that I'm living the first line of my obituary right now?" felt like Sorkin had peered into my brain and articulated a private creed. None of this is giving me any pleasure to admit.

What I'm saying is that I was like this even before I went to law school. I vibrated with the anxiety of wasted time. I enjoyed excessive volumes of reading. I knew my drive would misfire if I had nowhere to direct it. Everything bad that they tell you the law is going to do to your life, in other words, I figured I was already primed to accept. What's more, a legal career seemed premised on a worthy central bargain, albeit not the one that forms the punch line of lawyer jokes. I mean a bargain where you trade in less essential parts of yourself—casual hobbies, spare time, a few minor feelings—in exchange for a heightened ability to think and write and argue. This may be a fancy way of saying I was attracted to overwork (I was), or that I vibrated at a frequency that harmonized with the punishing tones of late capitalism (I did, and I still do). But the proposed trade seemed purer and more severe, even mystical. It wasn't about profit but about training to master a powerful system of argument. If all I had to give up for that grace were a few hours of sleep and some random pastimes, I'd be cheating myself if I *didn't* do it. This is the mechanism by which the law works, but also the way that I happened to approach the more difficult aspects of being a person: Cut away as much as you can get away with calling *unnecessary* and you'll be left with something that's basically functional.

Preparing to write the LSAT gave me my first opportunity to put my theory into practice. I kept the borders between study and the rest of my life discrete at first—I still read for pleasure, still wrote creatively, still saw friends. But as the exam drew closer, I began to experiment with leaving the valve open, letting the fumes seep into my life's other chambers and cloud them up one at a time. I wanted to test myself, see how much I could stand to renounce. The more of my life I could strip away and still function, the better my evidence that I was choosing the right future. Writing was the first to go, since splitting my attention in the run-up to the exam would have been a bad strategy. Six weeks from the test I abruptly withdrew from socializing. Four weeks out, I even gave up opening a book for fun, starving myself of narrative prose in the hopes that the LSAT's reading comprehension sections might begin to feel like an indulgence.

Deprived of connection and art and basically everything I'd ever loved—and desperately glorying in it—I couldn't always control where the beam of my focus shot off. I got fanatical about running, pretty much the only thing I still let myself do for fun. I developed a brief, forceful attraction to the tiny man with the staccato accent who gave me expert tips on the LSAT's logical reasoning sections, an emotional response that was neither logical nor reasonable. In the last few days before the test, I don't remember listening to any song apart from "Happy" by Pharrell, over and over, as if trying to convince myself of something. Grim, right? What's worse is that that shit actually worked. My days were etched in sharp focus. I was consistently hitting high scores on practice exams. When Pharrell sang "Clap along if you feel like happiness is the truth," I could hold forth obnoxiously on conditional logic, explaining what else you might infer from that statement about who was or wasn't clapping along and why. On the morning of the LSAT, I packed several pencils and a banana in a plastic baggie, went to the test center, and darkened a hundred Scantron bubbles from within the daze of a deep flow state. I had wagered that denying large segments of reality would make me feel powerful. For better and worse, I'd been right.

Denying large segments of reality is also what makes the law powerful. Though it nominally strives for justice, the "justice" of legal reasoning is more technical than what we usually use the word to mean in conversation. Protecting the vulnerable, redressing past wrongs, and rebalancing power are all things that may feel inherently just, depending on where you stand. But while the law happens to have done a lot to make these problems worse, equity is not the register in which it operates. A case may not take a defendant's race into account even though that might be crucial to the facts. Ditto a person's trauma history, or economic status, or various other points of disadvantage. Legal reasoning speaks the language of neutrality while coming down harder on the groups and people who have less power to fight it. You can only get to "neutral" at all by stripping away individuating factors—otherwise known as denying large segments of reality.

I thought my life would work exactly the way the law did. I would seek perfectibility within a closed system and shear off whatever I needed to in order to keep it running smoothly. When applied solely to me and my existence, that logic felt, at least at first, like freedom. But as I'd come to learn over the next three years, that principle was considerably harder for me to grasp when I was expected to wield it on the world.

ON BLACKOUT TUESDAY, the Law Society of Ontario issued a diversity statement, innocently as anything. It was the day on which individuals and corporations posted black squares to their social media accounts, a gesture more memorable for how it obscured activists' real-time messaging and organizing than for signaling a commitment to equity. "Today during Blackout Tuesday," the post read, "the Law Society supports and stands with our diversity partners and stakeholders to address the barriers faced by Black lawyers and paralegals in the fight to end discrimination." Like many of the groups on that day who posted statements, black squares, or some combination of the two, the Law Society did not have a spotless record. Its demographics tell a story that, while embarrassing, is far from unique to the legal industry. In its 2016 report, the Society surveyed the province's lawyers and found that only 3.2 percent were Black. The organization's more recent history, though, was on the nose in a way that made their words ring particularly false: nine months before Blackout Tuesday, the Society's governing board had voted against requiring every lawyer or paralegal "to adopt and abide by a statement of principles acknowledging their obligation to promote equality, diversity, and inclusion generally, and in their behavior towards colleagues, employees, clients, and the public." The suggestion that each licensee agree to at least *say* they're not racist was part of a suite of recommendations made by a working group that had been on the case since 2012. Their final report offered thirteen suggestions for beginning to remedy the profession's racism problem.

But item 3(1)—the statement of principles—was met with a wave of panicked outrage that the provision infringed lawyers' right to free speech. This discord engaged the field's familiar tension between professing to uphold a neutral value (free expression) by denying how justice actually works in the world (what racialized legal professionals must face, working amid the toxic combination of formalized social power, hefty capital, and too many white people).

A statement of principles is the emptiest gesture there is; its lack of action is right there in the name. Moreover, any burden the requirement imposed was negligible. Each person could draft their own statement and needn't even share it with the Law Society—merely confirm, on an annual basis, that they'd uphold it. They could write "I shalt not say the n-word (except when I sit with the partners in the company box at rap shows)" and they'd be golden. But as always, in the law, it was about the principle. Even this featherweight gesture of inclusion set people reciting a familiar set of right-wing talking points about compelled speech and thought policing. For a group of twenty-two lawyers running for the Law Society board, eliminating this "progressive agenda" was urgent enough to comprise their entire platform. Calling themselves "StopSOP," their website casts the statement of principles (SOP) as an act of intimidation; a sign of a profession "on the road to tyranny." Moreover, *they* were the victims, too, "called racists and bigots" by their crusading colleagues and offensively "mocked for being 'old white men'" (an allegation their site's profile page doesn't do much to disprove). In May 2019, Ontario and its 79.2 percent majority of white lawyers elected the StopSOP crew to the Law Society bench for a four-year term, where they repealed item 3(1), struck down a different motion that attempted to make the SOP entirely voluntary, and, when it was convenient to do so, posted the statement affirming diversity on Blackout Tuesday.

Rarely does the law flaunt its hypocrisy so clearly. In general, it elides politics and power differences in more slippery ways. "Every person is equal before and under the law," and all that. But the elemental fractures exposed by the SOP fiasco go down to the very bedrock of the profession. In a paper on the construction of "legal professionalism"—a core value of the field; there's a whole course on it in law school—historian Constance Backhouse describes how the concept "has been inextricably linked . . . to masculinity, whiteness, class privilege, and Protestantism." When the Law Society of Upper Canada was designing its first admissions tests in 1820, it aimed to weed out (white) applicants who were insufficiently "gentlemanly" by having them translate Cicero. Five years later, Cicero alone was no longer enough and they revamped the curriculum to mandate a full classical liberal education: "a general knowledge of English, Grecian and Roman History," familiarity with ancient Latin poetry and prose, and also—hey, why not—some math. They don't come out and say "only apply if you're white," but in 1820, they didn't have to. This value system trickles down into the contemporary makeup of the profession. It affects the types of arguments lawyers make in court, how cases get decided, which communities can access legal services, and who gets to go to law school at all.

I benefited from some of it, too. I can't tell you shit about Cicero but I did have a good liberal arts education and the financial solvency to pay for an LSAT course, which raised my odds of a good score and helped secure my acceptance into a highly ranked program. Moreover, when I applied I was still living at my parents' house and didn't have rent or similar major expenses, and my other responsibilities like part-time work were similarly light. There was little in my life I couldn't drop in order to study (with apologies to my friends; that was probably alarming).

The analogous governing body in the United States, the American Bar Association, manipulated the profession's demographics more directly. The ABA formally denied admission to Black people until 1943, when they resolved that "membership in the American Bar Association is not dependent upon race, creed, or color." All the while, they were seeking a greater diversity of white men by rolling back educational requirements—the opposite tactic from the Law Society of Upper Canada, but with an eye to the same uniformly racial result. In a journal article on the ABA's accreditation processes, scholar George B. Shepherd writes that these efforts were aimed at democratizing "an upper-class profession that unfairly denied entry to all except the wealthy and well connected." Even as Black lawyers were barred, the educational rollbacks tried to make the profession more accessible to poorer white people. And it worked! Abe Lincoln *taught himself* the law. His bar exam was oral and lasted only ten minutes. Now, in Illinois, the state where Lincoln practiced, writing the bar puts you out two days and $950, to say nothing of law school tuition; compared to some other states, $950 is a bargain. Though the ABA later abolished its explicitly racist practices, Shepherd writes, it kept up the discrimination under another name by "decreasing bar exam pass rates and tightening law school accreditation." Just as Black lawyers were entering the law in higher numbers, partly through new state schools and for-profit night schools, the ABA deemed those schools insufficient. It was well-known that they were the main entry points for Black legal professionals. This exclusion has trickled down as well: today, the ABA pledges commitments to diversity aimed at upping its percentage of Black members (which is currently at 5 percent across the United States) and yet, Shepherd shrugs that "the ABA's diversity efforts ring hollow" since they literally winnowed the color out themselves.

Looking beyond education and toward other corners of the legal system, this gap between blameless language and devastating real-world effects remains a common move. Consider how the Fourth Amendment nominally protects citizens against unreasonable search and seizure versus the provision's application in the 1996 case of *Whren v. United States*. In a unanimous decision authored by Justice

Antonin Scalia, the Supreme Court decided that minor traffic violations gave police broad discretion to search the offending vehicle (in which they may, as they did in *Whren*, find drugs). The ruling gave cops free rein to indulge their racial biases, letting them use traffic violations as a pretext for stopping whomever they suspected might be carrying drugs, and you don't need me to tell you what those people tended to look like. The petitioners in *Whren*, both of whom were Black, raised the possibility of racist overpolicing to the Court, which clapped back that the Fourth Amendment had nothing to do with racial bias. As Michelle Alexander writes, with palpable exasperation, in *The New Jim Crow*, "the Court barred any victim of race discrimination by the police *from even alleging a claim of racial bias*" under that amendment.

The state has a vested interest in ensuring a law is nominally decoupled from the reality of discrimination. The United States "actively promotes its supposed colorblindness," writes Keeanga Yamahtta-Taylor, as a way to justify rolling back legal protections against racism. If your society is no longer racist, why should there be laws that allow a claim of racial harm? This is also what the Supreme Court did with voting rights in 2013, Yamahtta-Taylor notes, when it struck down a key part of the Voting Rights Act and "essentially [ruled] that racism no longer hinders access" to casting a ballot. The holding is part of a broader network of policies that allow (and encourage) violent discrimination to persist. Harsh drug sentencing laws, long weaponized against Black people, lead to lengthy incarceration periods during which (and in many states, *after* which) people cannot vote. Slavery has been abolished but still exists under the Thirteenth Amendment as punishment for a crime; Jim Crow laws have been repealed, but racialized social control persists through policing and sentencing and housing discrimination; all the while, the law pays lip service to equal opportunity. I'm not breaking new ground by pointing any of this out—scholars, lawyers, and activists have been tracking these problems for decades—nor are these examples an exhaustive list. Where I'm going with it, though, is that when you're in training to enter the field, this is how they teach you to think. They're subtler about it, of course; they don't just up and say *today we're gonna learn how to do some racism*. They call it "thinking like a lawyer."

ON THE BASIS of my LSAT score and undergrad transcript, I was accepted to all of my prospective schools, including the University of Toronto Faculty of Law, where I ultimately chose to go. U of T had the nostalgia factor going for it—I'd also done my BA there— and it boasted a high job-placement rate. It also had the highest sticker price and the least forgiving financial aid policy of all the schools I'd applied to, and possibly in the whole country, but my ethic of denying reality was so comprehensive it extended, at least temporarily, to my finances.

On the first day of the degree, you're introduced to the case method. That method, the cornerstone of legal pedagogy, turns the reader into a kind of language filter that sifts through dense judicial prose to find the facts, the central issue, the outcome of the case, and—most importantly—the rule for which it stands. In the long self-own of trying to optimize everything about my life and future, I was thrilled that they were going to teach me a more efficient way to read. I was thrilled, more generally, just to be there. I signed up for too many extracurriculars because people said they were the best way to distinguish yourself in a high-performing class. I loved—as I'd known I would—not having to think about how to spend my time. I was either in class, transcribing lectures verbatim, or in the library, drenching my case books in highlighter. Some people also found time in which to be social, but I knew my limits. I only called my mom to ask if I should quit the program and work in a bookstore once, and that was during orientation week, so it didn't count. I had anticipated this hamster wheel, prepared and strategized for it. Now I was running. I got sick by week two, which felt like confirmation that I was working hard enough. Through it all, I kept banging on the door of the case method, which was more resistant than I'd expected. I could never locate the elusive rule. Presumably this was the thing I was paying thirty grand a year to be able to find.

This meant I was already falling behind. Pulling a rule from a case is merely the first step. The second phase—manipulating the relationship *between* cases—is both more demanding and more important. Any argument you craft is bound by the law's incremental development: you can't really make a point without citing its precedent in a previous case. The enterprising law student (which is to say, simply "the law student") also ought to be skilled at mapping the law over time; knowing how the court has ruled on similar questions in the past and predicting what that might mean for the next time the issue crops up. To work in a given legal area is to know the leading cases in your field, able to cite the authoritative ones at a moment's notice. Because the method looks to the past in order to build the future, it's tied to the mores and anxieties and conservatism of bygone eras, which makes major change difficult in the short term. The guiding logic is sameness rather than difference; you feed any narrative into the machine and it shaves the story down into the likeness of something that's already been decided by an earlier group of unelected white men.

My first struggles with this method were practical rather than ideological. I didn't yet think about the way the system could ruin other people's lives, only how it was ruining mine. I could stick my finger into a case and pull *something* out, but I couldn't tell you if it looked like a plum or like anything I had ever seen before, and I definitely couldn't base a coherent argument on that possible resemblance. Even at the time, I knew I couldn't be the only one experiencing this culture shock; if nothing else, my grades for exam-based courses were an indication of my thorough academic averageness. (Marks, in law school, are often based on a single exam worth 100 percent of your grade, which is then plotted on a curve of high achievers; these grades, in turn, have a hand in determining your early job prospects.) But I could only get to being average at all by teaching myself principles by brute-force rote. I couldn't properly grasp legal reasoning until I understood its foundations; as I scrabbled there at the bottom, more concepts were piled on top of the basics, all of which I'd have to climb eventually.

Part of the reason this logical method felt so invisible is because it was made to be. The first-year curriculum has students reading and arguing law without pausing to talk about what the law is or means, or what parts of the fact pattern—like social or political context—the decision may have omitted. It's like waking up one day and agreeing to abide by a collective delusion, but only deducing the rules by watching those around you obey, rather than being allowed to ask what they are. The law school, especially in first year, is a pedagogical bubble. Maybe there's a seminar you can take in upper years that touches on these more conceptual questions. But you don't really see or discuss the effects of legal reasoning until you're out in the world talking all fancy, trying to put your principles into practice without ruining anyone's life.

Eventually, I did see somebody acknowledge and explain this frustrating invisibility. But it didn't happen in law school, or anywhere near the degree at all. It came from a book I wasn't looking for in a city I didn't live in, when I happened to be visiting the summer after first year. *The Alchemy of Race and Rights: Diary of a Law Professor*, by legal scholar Patricia J. Williams, is a key text of critical race theory. Critical race theory, or CRT, is the body of thought that explores how systems like the law encode marginalization as part of their practice. Back then I'd never heard of CRT; though the phrase (and a wildly inaccurate definition of it) is presently dividing the United

States along a new axis, they didn't teach it in my law school at the time. I'd learned about Williams in a random footnote from Claudia Rankine's *Citizen;* since *Alchemy* hasn't been reissued since its publication in 1992, I thought I'd spend forever tracking it down. Instead, I found it waiting for me on a used bookstore shelf in the midsummer swelter of Ithaca, New York. I was there to visit someone I'd just started seeing in Toronto, who was taking the same summer critical-theory course Patricia Williams had taken when she wrote the essay she later expanded into *Alchemy.* Finding the book was disorientingly easy after I'd steeled myself for so much more difficulty, which was also how it felt to make room for another person in my life. If I met someone, I figured they'd have to be a law student purely out of convenience—who had time for anything else? But Philip, thankfully, wasn't. While he spent six weeks reading psychoanalytic theory, I bummed around downtown Ithaca, reading Patricia Williams.

This is another way of saying that critical race theory was so far beyond the ambit of my law school curriculum that I had to fall in love, spend twelve hours on two different Greyhounds, and traverse the Canada-U.S. border to even learn what it was. (These days, with the right-wing attack against an incoherent specter of CRT as unpatriotic "race-based ideology," this southward pilgrimage to discover it seems somewhat more fantastical.) The absence of these ideas in the program makes sense given the University of Toronto's proximity to Bay Street, the heart of the country's corporate market. U of T is basically a feeder for the Big Law firms that line the city's financial corridor and, while those spaces could certainly use more cultural competency, from a purely pragmatic standpoint, teaching critical race theory is a waste of time. So, I didn't go into the degree expecting some kind of wildly progressive education. But, after a year of failing to understand the material, I was still relieved to see somebody finally admit legal reasoning has gaping holes in it.

Now, in the post–Blackout Tuesday world, they apparently teach

critical race theory as part of the law school's mandatory professionalism seminars. I should add that this only raises the bar about an
inch off the floor—such meetings are called *compulsory* but are sched-
uled during lunch breaks, last about an hour, and at least when I took
them, weren't framed in a way that connected to the contents of our
other classes. But they also sound generally better than the ethics and
professionalism modules I attended in first year. In those sessions,
you showed up for a slice of cold pizza and to listen as the modera-
tor led a discussion on the proper tension for a handshake, or how
to avoid getting defensive with your peers when asked to check your
privilege. These are not on-the-nose hypotheticals but actual examples from the notes I took as I grimly chewed my pizza. The University of Toronto's law student–run paper, *Ultra Vires*, reported on one
of these virtual CRT sessions in January 2021. The workshop leader,
the director of antiracism and cultural diversity at the University of
Toronto, asked the attendees to offer examples of intersectionality
"within the Black Lives Matter movement." In the chat, an administrator of the law school suggested "african-american cops' roles," as if
policing were an identity or an axis of oppression. When concerned
students started sending messages asking her to at least explain what
she meant by that, *Ultra Vires* says, she allegedly did not reply.

I'VE READ THE first chapter of the *The Alchemy of Race and Rights*
so many times, I can recite the opening from memory: "Since subject position is everything in my analysis of the law, you deserve to
know that it's a bad morning. I am very depressed." Williams is sitting in bed, wearing a ratty terrycloth bathrobe and reading about
contract law, fielding relatable thoughts like "I *hate* being a lawyer."
She's grappling with a Louisiana case from 1835, *Icar v. Suars*, about
flaws in merchandise for which a buyer might seek a refund. In *Icar*,
the defective merchandise in question—and a contributing factor

to Williams's general mood and attitude toward her job—is an enslaved Black woman named Kate. The "flaw" is that she tried to run away. Keep in mind that this is not a case that frames itself as being about slavery or racist violence. It's ostensibly about the much more practical question of whether a dude can get his money back. The question for the court to resolve: based on her actions, is Kate "crazy [or] only stupid"? Only the former would secure a refund.

The court eventually rules in the plaintiff's favor, concluding that "the buyer would not have purchased with a knowledge of the vice. We are satisfied that the slave in question was wholly, and perhaps worse than, useless." While I'm sure there'd be a caveat about the case's horrifying circumstances, in legal pedagogy, this case would probably be taught for its principle: how a bad product can invalidate a contract. As a teaching tool, its lesson comes so neatly packaged— buyer is inconvenienced and gets cash back—textured by an unusual, if inhumane, question (is Kate's behavior something that a buyer should reasonably have been able to anticipate?). I wouldn't be surprised if a similar hypothetical has turned up on an exam in the past twenty years. In 2018, after all, a University of Texas first-year constitutional law exam asked students to relitigate *Brown v. Board of Education*, arguing for the pro-segregation side sixty-four years after they lost. The facts in *Icar* are apt to stir, in students primed for both-sidesism, a similar itch for devil's advocacy. This is what legal reasoning does.

What legal reasoning *doesn't* do is talk about what the case leaves out. The case method considers certain facts—like Kate's humanity under inhumane conditions—as irrelevant because, to contract law, they are. Ignoring her personhood is a natural outcome of a system that extracts neutral rules from empirical messes (especially in Louisiana in 1835). As the rules that govern our social reality, the law has no truck with power. The system *must* standardize reality in order for its rules to fit. Arguing the *facts* of the case, and their social and legal implications, is part of a lawyer's job. But Kate was never going to get a lawyer.

By focusing on her own "craziness"—her depression, her "hair stream[ing] wildly and the eyes rolling back in [her] head"—Williams aligns herself with Kate, another Black woman "trying to decide if she is stupid or crazy." But the comparison heightens the contrast: Williams can articulate her fury at the law and still be read as a scholar. Not so for Kate. This is what critical race theory does: it retells old narratives and highlights the exclusions they were trying to pass off as natural, often by way of first-person stories like Williams's. The rule of law, in critical race theory, is a story white supremacy tells itself. It acknowledges the gulf between what the law says and what it hopes to achieve, whom it hopes to keep in power versus whom it plans to disenfranchise. Conservative legal scholars—and now that it's gone mainstream, just conservatives—villainize the theory for the way it muddies the hem of Lady Justice. I imprinted on it for the same reason. Williams's work, and the work of others writing in this tradition, was tactile in a way I could actually understand. Of course, people had made this world up out of words. Of course, they had their weaknesses and biases. But why didn't we ever touch on this stuff in the classroom? We talked about the law like it was a perfectly made object that had no seams. But its joints were loose if you knew where to look.

More than the fact that I could actually understand it, part of what made CRT so thrilling to read, as a young law student, was that its voice and its form were the opposite of what I'd been taught were acceptable in first-year legal writing and professionalism. "It is a bad morning, I am very depressed" may have described how it felt to walk into a law classroom, but it wasn't how you were supposed to argue while you sat in one. *Alchemy* gave me permission to start thinking differently. You were allowed to use first-person pronouns? You could admit that you were exhausted? Legal language, Williams writes, "flattens and confines in absolutes the complexity of meaning inherent in any given problem." It suggests that the world should be shaped by universal legal truths, and that those truths were spoken into existence by "objective, 'unmediated' voices." We know now, of course, that they were neither unmediated nor objective; they were white, male, and invested in staying on top. Explained this way, in this moment, a mere two years after the forty-fifth president fanned a moral panic over critical race theory, it sounds hopelessly obvious. But law school, especially in the first year, is such a hermetic environment that this sort of thing can feel impossible to remember. After a year of getting lost in abstract principles, it was tempting to ask, but easy to understand, why on earth they'd been hiding this stuff from me.

I DON'T MEAN to suggest that I was the only person in a class of two hundred who had anything resembling a social conscience. There were spaces in the program that exposed me to members of my cohort who were committed to public-interest work: upper-year courses on racial politics and law; legal clinics; student clubs. But by then, I was too closed off and in my head to reach out to other people. I felt a sense of unease that existing student organizations didn't really offer an outlet for. Clubs at the law school were generally divisible into three buckets: those that claimed affinity on the basis of an identity category (like Out in Law for LGBTQ students, or the Muslim Law Students Association), those that did so on the basis of interest (the Venture Capital Law Society, the Environmental Law Club), and those that served as last-ditch attempts to maintain a connection with some kind of nonlaw pursuit (the Law Poets Society; In Vino Veritas, the wine appreciation club; the a cappella group, The Supreme Chords, which I joined in my first year).

But the kind of affinity I was looking for didn't seem to exist.

Though the a cappella group was among the kindest spaces I encountered in the entire program, I could never totally relax. *What if we end up on opposite sides of a deposition one day?* I thought as we worked out intricate harmonies to "Wrecking Ball." (I'm sure lots of people wonder this in law school; maybe the dissonance is something the heavy drinking culture helps smooth over.) The point of the group was to bond over something non–law related, but in a culture that encouraged the competitive shedding of life weight, nothing felt exactly like leisure. We approached our musical commitments with the same life-or-death rigor that law students bring to everything else. While this meant that we had some fire harmonies, it also meant skipping rehearsal seemed like it might tank your career. The thing that I'd longed for back when I was bingeing legal dramas had finally come to pass: there was nothing in my life that didn't bend toward the goal of professionalism. There was no wasted time. It probably won't surprise you to learn that was untenable. After first and second year, all I wanted was a space I could sneak into and announce, "It is a bad morning, and I am very depressed."

"It cannot be denied that the university is a place of refuge," Fred Moten and Stefano Harney write in *The Undercommons*, "and it cannot be accepted that the university is a place of enlightenment. In the face of these conditions one can only sneak into the university and steal what one can." The authors aren't mounting a specific case about the law school, but a number of things they criticize the institution for overvaluing—professionalization, isolation, rationality, a complacency toward leaving the world as it is—are so central to legal education that they often get codified in its curriculum. As an alternative, Harney and Moten advocate a way of being in the university that's grounded in study and collective critique. To be "in but not of" the place, to use their phrasing, is to be present within it but an outlaw from its value system. To steal what you need in order to build a kind of freedom. Patricia Williams stole the case method to invert the law's fixation with neutrality. I stole the lunch budget to start a reading group.

At our first session of the Race and Law reading group, nearly thirty people showed up, many of whom seemed drawn for deeper reasons than "lunch will be provided." Though I'd pitched it across various faculties, the majority of them *were* law students, mostly first-years. That thrilled me: perhaps they needed reassurance, still in the first fever of the case method, that eventually they'd remember there were other ways to think. We read Saidiya Hartman, Robin Kelley, Frank Wilderson, Simone Browne. Names you don't often see on law school syllabi but whose books kept me tethered in my fraying final year. The attendance dropped off pretty steeply after that first session, but a core group of us would still meet every month to talk about what we'd read. Often, we were just exhausted, and said as much. I'm grateful to those students for showing up every month to help me create something I couldn't find anywhere else. To my knowledge, the sessions didn't continue after I left the program. I'm at peace with that; I didn't expect anyone to take on the labor of running it and was never sure anyone even needed it as much as I did. The aim wasn't to transform the program—literally who cares—but just to find more livable spaces inside it. To dwell in the stories our education would technically consider irrelevant. To wonder, in asking these questions, whether the law would call us stupid or crazy.

The group adjourned a few weeks out from exams. It was the end of my third and final year and I still hadn't found a job. After second year, I hadn't summered at a law firm; when I struck out at OCIs, I unsuccessfully applied to a different round of employers before eventually taking a faculty research-assistant job. Now, a year later, I'd struck out a second time during the interview process for articling, the ten-month apprenticeship period students must complete before they get licensed in Canada. I could have tried harder, because in law you can always try harder. But I'd started sabotaging myself a little, too. In an articling interview with a criminal defense firm (not the pro-cop firm I mentioned earlier) I missed a clear opening to profess the requisite distaste for work-life balance. "We'll call you at all hours," my interviewer said. "Because that's the job, right?" Feeling uncharacteristically belligerent, I went off-script and refused to agree. I left the building ten minutes later, carrying my heels and weeping in relief.

My grades were probably what did me in. They reflected my very basic inability to bridge the gap between the world the law described and the world that truly existed. It wasn't out of principles or politics that my arguments fell apart—I knew going in that the law was racist as hell, even if I couldn't have told you all the ways—it was because I truly couldn't get my head around the case method. Trying to impose it on the way I think and read and write never stopped feeling like the most basic peg/hole mismatch, blunt and futile. I'm sure I would have eventually worn the edges off if I'd stuck with the law, kept trying to force it, learned on the job. But after spending so long fetishizing the clean architecture of legal reasoning, it felt like a slap to be repeatedly told, across case briefs and research essays and exam answers, how much I still wasn't getting it. On my assignments, professors would compliment me on how elegantly I summarized the facts of a case. That's like saying "at least you didn't kill anyone" if you didn't get a client off.

I also didn't do myself any favors by ignoring the increasingly desperate messages from the career office. They were understandably twitchy about my failure to secure or report a job. I was, too. But they kept close tabs on us, the unemployed stragglers who skewed the school's job stats and future donation prospects. They also claimed to offer guidance for people who wanted out of law and to put their degree to use in a different field. Persuaded by the latter, I booked a meeting to ask what else people had done with this degree that could supposedly do anything; what else the first line of my obituary might say if not "lawyer." The career officer mentioned a single graduate who'd gone into journalism, but the rest of the meeting was just us shrugging at each other and saying things like, "Politics?"

By the end of the program, there wasn't much of me left, a corrupted version of what I'd uncarefully wished for. The degree didn't make me sharp and hard and powerful. It gave me a clarity of purpose that propelled me for three years, but it also made me soft and miserable. I graduated but didn't write the bar exam, a decision that still confuses people several years later. I had to explain it to a dentist last month. Relatives who remember that I earned the degree still stumble when I remind them that I voluntarily stepped off the path. I took a coffee meeting with the graduate who'd gone into journalism, and even after I said I'd been out of school for a year and had no interest in practicing, she spent our conversation trying to convince me to write the bar exam "just so you can say you did it." In my follow-up thank-you note, I sent her a viral essay I'd published about how law school had mangled my ability to read for pleasure. I never heard from her again.

THE LAW SCHOOL I see now isn't the one I graduated from four years ago. The people who will go on to shape jurisprudence seem wiser than the ones of the past. They understand the violence of neutrality and appear more committed to closing the gap between the word of law and how it gets enacted. Maybe, in a hundred years, people will see the results. In the lunchtime professionalism training sessions of my cohort, where we talked about privilege disclaimers and handshake strength, it's probably good that CRT was never on the menu. If by some grim joke my class, famed even among the faculty's cutthroat cohorts for our careerism, had heard a high-ranking white person said something iffy, I suspect it would have been par for the course. It might even have been one of the students who said it. But the class of 2023 decided to write an open letter.

Addressed to the dean, the letter's a sharp and knowing piece of advocacy: it gives an economical recap of the facts; clearly explains, point by point, the issues at stake in the administrator's comment about Black cops as an intersectional identity; connects those broader issues to the myriad failures of action within the law school; is confident and stylish enough to indulge in the occasional barb ("A cursory look at the demographic makeup of our class reveals the administration's failures to seriously act on their commitments to anti-racism"); and brings it all home with four calls to action. The next round of professionalism training sessions ought to use it as a teaching tool. In fewer than seven hundred words, it reveals more about the realities of legal doctrine than three years of law school ever did for me.

What We Want and When We Want It

On May 4, 1969, civil rights leader James Forman interrupted a Sunday service at Manhattan's Riverside Church and began to deliver the Black Manifesto. From the pulpit, Forman issued the core demand: $500 million in reparations from white Christian churches and Jewish synagogues. This cool half billion was ostensibly a lowball; Detroit's National Black Economic Development Conference (BEDC), for whom Forman spoke, had conservatively estimated that there were thirty million Black people living in the United States. By that metric, each person's payout would be a measly fifteen dollars. But a modest symbolic sum was an acceptable first step—this was just the opening salvo in a multi-stage program to redress centuries of exploitation; the U.S. government and private enterprise, the proposal implies, were next up. "We are no longer afraid to demand our full rights as a people in this decadent society," Forman intoned, as the church pastor urged the organist to play loudly enough to drown him out. The pipes didn't matter—Forman's words had other channels to the public. A couple months later, the full text of his speech was published in the *New York Review of Books*. America, it seemed, was listening.

When it came to seeking reparations, religious organizations were an attractive target for several reasons. They had money, for one, their coffers topped up by wealthy white donors and friends in high places. (The construction for Riverside, a soaring neo-Gothic edifice, had been funded by John D. Rockefeller, the richest person in American history.) But more significantly, these institutions were also complicit in the spread of slavery, colonialism, and racial capitalism. White Christian churches and Jewish synagogues had "aided and abetted . . . the exploitation of colored peoples around the world"; among other things, Forman and the BEDC wanted Black people to recognize how Christianity's "hypocritical declarations and doctrines of brotherhood [have] abused our trust and faith." They called for widespread civil disobedience in places of worship across the United States. Following the initial demand for $500 million in funds, the manifesto sets out a list itemizing how the monies will be spent: developing a Southern Land Bank, Black-owned and operated publishing houses, Black-controlled TV broadcasters, research and training centers, welfare and strike funds, and a university. The white-owned versions of those institutions weren't doing any special magic for representation—TV stations, in particular, were cited for being mostly racist "propaganda"—but asking them to pivot to positivity wouldn't have fixed things. No matter how well-meaning the outlet, guilt and goodwill have a ceiling. Put power in the hands of the disenfranchised and watch it flow to new heights.

It's a thrilling list, ambitious in its scope and vigorous in its repeated insistence that these are but "small demands." Though the document repeatedly acknowledges the paltriness of the payout at the per-person scale, the demand isn't really about the unit of the singular person at all, but about envisioning a secure, actionable future for the community. It was certainly about the money—the sum of $500 million is repeatedly invoked in full, a string of zeroes trailing in its wake, to considerable effect—but the stony refrain of fifteen dollars also underlined all that they *weren't* asking for. Thinking at the scale of the collective is central to Black radical movements. As historian Robin D. G. Kelley writes in *Freedom Dreams: The Black Radical Imagination*, the reparations proposals of such groups tend to "focus less on individual payments than on securing funds to build autonomous black institutions." By the late 1960s, the Black Manifesto was far from the only reparations call in circulation; the Panthers had one built into their platform, as did the Nation of Islam. But even among these, the breadth of the BEDC's proposal was unique: It was, Kelley writes, "the first systematic, fully elaborated plan for reparations to emerge from the black freedom movement."

Despite the imaginative force behind the demands, the response by religious communities did not match the manifesto's sweeping vision. Though some religious leaders were moved to help, their contributions often involved pouring more dollars into preexisting church-run support programs rather than giving new capital to Black-owned initiatives. It was less politically risky for them to pick and choose which parts of the demand they wanted to respond to—which ignores the point of a demand—than go all-in for justice. Well-meaning gestures, like handing out a few more grants to community organizations, gave churches and synagogues a way to look like they were, at the very least, not so racist that they opposed the freedom struggle altogether. But, more importantly, it didn't rock the boat. Churches owed their resources to wealthy, conservative donors. John D. Rockefeller, the richest guy in America and a reliable philanthropic pipeline, likely didn't build his oil monopoly while also being sympathetic to causes like Black liberation. Many a milder revolutionary impulse has been crushed for fear of pissing off a wealthy white donor.

One written response to the Manifesto, issued by the Executive Council of the Episcopal Church, tries very hard to have it both ways. Their reply acknowledges that systemic racism is a problem and that they "have begun to listen," yet in the same breath say they "do not accept the Manifesto as it is presented." After itemizing the money they've already allocated toward social-justice initiatives, the letter concludes that "the central contribution of the Christian Church to the crisis in our society cannot be measured simply in terms of money." This seems awfully convenient. Their preferred metric is the human spirit, which they strengthen "by affirming and practicing—in word and action, *and as well with money*—the spirit of reconciliation" (emphasis mine). In a handy little sleight-of-tongue, the Executive Council institutes a tiny schism between the concepts of *action* and *reparations*. The manifesto offers a choice between two options—pay up or shut up—but the Council splinters the dichotomy into a third (love thy neighbor, but make it budget). In the schema of the Black Manifesto, money *is* action; it's the only currency that will allow Black communities to build an equitable and sustainable future. But the Church swaps that out for easy, cheap alternatives. Like tending to the human spirit. Or *listening*. This seems like precisely the kind of hypocritical declarations and doctrines of brotherhood the BEDC objected to in the first place.

The demand is a necessary genre, but also—as the Executive Council Response shows—a limited one. A demand draws attention, often in a manner that's highly visible and disruptive, to a gap between the unjust world as it is and the more equitable way it ought to be—especially when the latter is being ignored or falsely advertised. It is a call for institutions to embody their stated values, a public challenge for them to do what they say and pay what they owe. But the demand is also finite in what it can achieve. For one thing, it's hard to enforce. Churches could just shrug and say they tried, or ignore it altogether. More importantly, though, the demand must be phrased very carefully. It might ask for improvement from a system for which that's the wrong question. To demand better means *better* is something an institution is capable of, or deserves our help in becoming. But what if the rot goes all the way down? You can demand evidence of change, like representative demographics, but that won't do much if the whole edifice is built on white supremacy. Now, the genre is even sprouting across the political spectrum, with reactionary open letters and anodyne collective statements jostling for attention alongside demands more faithful to the form's radical roots. Everyone can't be worth giving into just because they put their foot down.

IT IS NOT in my nature to be unyielding. I put on different voices when the situation calls for it and turned that into a job. I irritate my editors with my tendency to equivocate. Some personalities possess a force that propels them outward; mine does the opposite, the target for my fury and critique always on my own chest. If in a low-stakes situation, like what to have for dinner, I assert a preference that's directly oppositional to yours, here's a tip: Ask me again in five minutes. It's not timidity, exactly, but more like a cost-saving measure. Certain types of conflict strike me as a waste of time and energy, and I will sooner inconvenience myself by going around them. Part of this is nurture: I grew up an eldest daughter in a house of strong personalities and was socialized to accommodate. Made to feel unwelcome in the city of my childhood, I developed certain strategies to minimize my presence or my difference. I may also, as collateral damage, have forgotten what my face looks like. Of course, I have convictions. Out here trying to make a living, I run into them like brick walls and it hurts like hell. I just prefer not to spend time explaining those convictions to other people until the situation calls for it.

I need to be very careful that this interpersonal preference does not become, at larger scales, something like apoliticism. Being part of an avowed collective is one thing; when you show up to march and demand, your voice joins in to strengthen that of the group. But if the people you're demanding something from have only let in *one* of you, it can be harder to raise your voice. Your acceptance may feel implicitly conditional on your silence. If you're the only one with a transformative vision in an all-white classroom or department or office or masthead, solo agitating could just as easily get you marked as a problem.

Popular culture feeds us this trope over and over: The solo demander is a threat to social order. Never mind progressiveness—their cause isn't even always political. Hostage-takers make demands. So do terrorists. In the musical adaptation of *The Phantom of the Opera*, André and Firmin, the beleaguered new management of the Palais Garnier, get peppered with increasingly menacing letters from the self-styled "O.G." (Opera Ghost). The Phantom demands, among other things, a salary, control over casting, and general adherence to "how [his] theatre is to be run." "Should these commands be ignored," the final note warns, "a disaster beyond your imagination will occur." (*Phantom* was the first musical I ever saw; at five years old, this threat, issued in Colm Wilkinson's tremulous tenor, absolutely terrified me.) There are no politics at play here, apart from petty workplace ones. The Opera Ghost is pissed about how much André and Firmin suck up to the opera's prima donna and that they persistently refuse to cast his crush, Christine, in the lead role. The Phantom's agenda is aesthetic: Your opera is shit; make it better or people will die. A few songs later, after a show that ignored his directions, the Phantom delivers on his promise and brings the Palais's chandelier crashing down on the audience.

The demand is also a trope of cinematic hostage situations—in *The Dark Knight*, the Joker broadcasts a video of himself torturing a man in a Batman costume, issuing a challenge for the real Batman to please stand up or risk a higher body count; in Spike Lee's heist film *Inside Man*, in which a group of hostage-takers (with more overtly political motives) occupy a Wall Street bank, their escalating demands start with a very practical call for pizza and scale up from there. These may feel like quirky examples, but their existence and visibility set up an important context: when faced with the demands of radical collectives, the state often invokes the rhetoric of violence and threat that characterize this type of terroristic situation. It's a popular, bad-faith way to shore up power: make it look like there's parity between people seeking basic human rights and hostage-takers seeking to bring down the chandelier of democracy.

At other times, the demand becomes an expression of virtue. People with sufficient power might phrase their good intentions as an imperative—which, while well-meaning, may be an awkward vehicle for change. This is what Frances McDormand did at the 2018 Oscars, in her Best Actress acceptance speech for her turn in *Three Billboards Outside Ebbing, Missouri*. After asking the female nominees across all Oscar categories to stand up, McDormand closed her speech with the following mic drop: "I have two words to leave with you tonight, ladies and gentlemen: *Inclusion. Rider*." The term launched a thousand frenzied Google searches from viewers at home who had no idea what that meant. An inclusion rider, it turns out, is a contractual provision that actors—ones with enough star and bargaining power—can demand before signing onto a project.

Stacy L. Smith, founder of the Annenberg Inclusion Initiative—a California-based think tank that studies film-industry inequality and that published the 2019 report on a more inclusive vision for animation—introduced the concept in a 2014 column for *The Hollywood Reporter*. Demanding that equity be written into the contract, Smith explained, could look like a clause "[stating] that tertiary speaking characters should match the gender distribution of the setting for the film, as long as it's sensible for the plot." Admittedly, this is the first time the idea of such riders reached the public, and the discourse of gender and racial justice in 2014 was a lot less robust than it is today. That said, this is an oddly conservative example from somebody who leads a think tank on inequality. It stakes its claim in faithfulness to a film's verisimilitude and the vision (and conscience) of its creatives, rather than any a priori sense of justice or restitution. It seems, in other words, deferent to and loathe to piss off powerful people. Similar to how McDormand (and much of the industry discourse that followed) framed the representation question, Smith's example is only concerned with greater visibility for "women and girls," which means cis white women and cis white girls. In a template for inclusion riders, co-authored by Smith and released four years later, in the wake of McDormand's speech, the categories have been revised and expanded to also contemplate people of color, people with disabilities, and LGBTQ people.

These omissions indicate a more basic problem: the celebrity rider, the former territory of zany backstage snack demands, is—despite the crusading spirit of McDormand's call to action—a clumsy vehicle for demanding fixes to a broken industry. It puts the onus for transforming the system in the hands of a few well-meaning white people, and then only if they happen to feel like it. Chances are, most of them never will, as they have a vested interest in maintaining an order that skews heavily, yet precariously, in their favor. Like a church that relies on donations from wealthy and conservative patrons, actors have a strong disincentive to stand up to career-making industry executives on a good day. They can't even be relied on to object in the face of a wrong as patently objectionable as violent, systematic sexual abuse. Nobody with that big a conflict of interest should be put in the driver's seat for change. Hollywood is too far gone, despite the consciences of McDormand and others working inside it. Their demands can only do so much.

After Oscar night, the uptake of inclusion riders was predictably spotty. The outcome has less to do with the principle than its proposed implementation: while quotas are one way to start a possible journey toward equity, things can get dicey if the affirmative action depends solely on individual whim and benevolence. (Though, as the history of affirmative action also makes clear, things can get dicey even if they depend on more stable-looking systems, like institutional policy or even the Supreme Court.) The film and TV industries have tried to find ways to put equity riders into practice more effectively: in the past few years, the BBC committed to a cast and crew, across all of their programming, of which at least 20 percent would come from underrepresented backgrounds or identities. This is still far from a comprehensive form of equality—lumping every "other" identity into the same 20 percent still makes for a pretty white, male, cisgender, able-bodied production. Moreover, according to the U.K.'s Department for Work and Pensions' 2018/2019 survey, 19 percent of the adult population alone identify as people with a disability, which fills up that quota pretty quickly—but in terms of inclusion, it moves the dial more than one guy who's been guilted into asking, in his new blockbuster flick, for a few more tertiary talking females. Like animation's efforts to attract and retain minoritized talent, these attempts still proceed from the assumption that the production is white-run—they get to keep creative control, and everyone else gets let in under a special provision.

The inclusion rider, appended to a contract, reminds us that demands can also fall under the ambit of the law. A contract establishes a set of expectations that, if breached, give rise to certain actions (or demands). Prior to suing somebody, one party may send the other a demand letter outlining a claim to payment or some other outcome. Before I had an accurate idea of what legal practice was, the demand shaped the way that I imagined all lawyers communicated all the time. As someone not prone to demanding, this was not off-putting but actually very attractive. I wanted to *demand* the state release my client and *demand* the prosecution hand over the discovery material and *demand* the jury find them not guilty, as if the job were license to forgo politeness. This is a horrible way to think about being a person, let alone a lawyer. It is, however, a decent way to think about our right to protest. It's more favorably looked upon for institutions to demand actions of individuals (pay taxes, pay tuition, don't ask questions) than for us to revolt and reject those terms. But, as history has shown, sometimes civil disobedience is the best course of action.

Reversing the terms and issuing a collective demand is also, too often, the cue for liberal institutions to cry that they're being attacked. Further to the right, conservatives often frame the action as synonymous with emotional frailty. These two positions represent the rough historical trajectory of political responses to the demand: from overreading it as a credible threat to writing it off as the whingeing of coddled minds. Both are self-serving, and both miss the point—the former by inflating the demand's power and the latter by minimizing it.

THE LIST OF demands has deep roots in 1960s and 1970s student activism. That period involved a series of protracted, significant social shifts—the Vietnam War was ongoing, climate anxiety was rising, racial violence was everywhere—and the gulf between the world as it was and the one that universities hawked in their messaging was infuriatingly apparent to their students. They asserted that social-justice issues weren't marginal to the schools' operations, but realities—lived both within and outside the ivory tower—for which it was culpable and accountable. As an enlightened society in miniature, the university failed to live up to the ideals it professed. As a microcosm of a white supremacist state riddled with racism and ethically dubious financial commitments, it was more successful.

College demographics were changing, with more Black and racialized students filling the incoming classes year-over-year. But comparable changes in curriculum or faculty demographics were slower, if they existed at all. The difference between the glacial drip of curricular change and rapid shifts in the student makeup made a different type of hypocrisy possible: a school could point to its student body as evidence of successful diversity initiatives while doing nothing to nurture or enshrine such diversity. Students reacted to this complacency across decades and campuses. At UC Berkeley in 1960, the Afro-American Student Union (AASU) demanded a self-governed Black Studies department on the basis that, as the proposal states in all caps, "WHAT IS GOOD FOR WHITE PEOPLE IS OFTENTIMES WORSE THAN BAD FOR US." In answer, the chancellor approved a Black Studies program, but one that would live within a preexisting department (which ignored the demand for autonomy) and be implemented by a committee that didn't contain any Black staff or students (which was just bad decision-making). As with the Black Manifesto, which was vexing religious leaders across the country at around the same time, the goal wasn't just resources—*you wanted some funds, there you go*—but the power to turn them into something self-sustaining. Like the church, the university panicked at the specter of change and tried to dial it back. The AASU rejected the chancellor's offer and called a strike alongside other minoritized student groups. Police were installed on the campus and, later, the National Guard. This was not the last example of a military offensive launched against campus protest, nor the most devastating—a year later, at Kent State University and Jackson State University, the National Guard shot and killed multiple students engaged in peaceful action.

This physical ferocity has been matched by political aggression. Politicians, business leaders, and administrators band together and issue demands of their own, doubling down on their refusal to redistribute power. After the Kent and Jackson State tragedies, Richard Nixon convened the President's Commission on Campus Unrest, a group that spent several months looking into the "history and causes" of student protest, and published their findings in a four-hundred-page report. The investigation pitched itself as an act of due diligence after the National Guard murders, but it's evident a few pages in that the Commission had a very different agenda. "The crisis on American campuses has no parallel in the history of the nation," the report opens, moaning like a death knell. They "fear new violence and growing enmity" from a generation "that opposes all that is traditional and dignified." The portraiture only gets more absurd from there, painting student activists as dangerously intolerant of differing views and the slow pace of change. The unexpected star of the report's early pages is the word *diversity*, which becomes, through some fancy sentence work, a civic right under grave threat. Students must "recognize that they are citizens of a nation which was founded on tolerance and diversity, and they must become more understanding of those with whom they differ"—to do otherwise, the report says, is to threaten democracy. This use of *diversity* foreshadows the path the word would cut through the courts a few years later, when it was transformed into a preemptive defense against reverse discrimination. Nixon, with his skill for ramping up civil rights discourse into punitive state control, was fluent in this kind of lip service.

Decades later, these strategies haven't really changed. This is still the same tool kit that powerful institutions reach for when they're freaked out by protest: Casting people who advocate for social justice as the ones who are *really* "intolerant of diversity." Slyly invoking the hostage milieu by describing the demand like it's dangerous, even criminal. Nixon established an entire committee, made them work for three months, and had them churn out an incredible volume of words, all to make student protestors out to be the *real* bad guys. He ought to have calmed down a little; stopped mistaking conflict for abuse. Student protest unsettled powerful institutions—which is good! That's what it set out to do. But university admin and government representatives—joined, on Nixon's report, by cops, lawyers, and centrist media—didn't like being made to feel unsettled. Sensing a threat to their dominance, the commission recast that peaceful protest as a form of violence. Having sufficiently exaggerated what they were up against, they looked more vindicated in responding with extreme measures, like sending in the troops. The report was not an apology for the killings at Kent and Jackson State—it was an apologia.

Decades later, college administrators keep misreading the student demand to suit their worldviews. In 2015, following the Ferguson uprisings, another period of coordinated student action swept across U.S. campuses. At the forefront was "Concerned Student 1950," a collective at the University of Missouri, whose name is a reference to the year the first Black student was admitted to the college. The group sent a list of demands to the administration, chief among them the immediate removal of Tim Wolfe, the university president, and a formal apology in which he admitted to both his privilege and the existence of systemic oppression. The latter seems like a low bar, especially given how cursory copping to one's privilege has become, but he had a hard time clearing it. "Tim Wolfe, what do you think systematic oppression is?" a protestor asked him in a parking lot after a fundraiser. Earlier that day, Wolfe had issued an apology for the racist incidents at Missouri, but nothing more. "Systematic oppression," Wolfe shoots back, with the doomed overconfidence of a white man who's just raised a boatload of money, "is because you don't believe that you have the equal opportunity for success." *What?* "Did you just blame *us* for systematic oppression, Tim Wolfe?" the student asks, her voice raw with disbelief. "Did you just blame *Black students?*"

IN LAW SCHOOL, I enrolled in what was then the only course on racial politics the faculty offered. (The course calendar suggests they've expanded their offerings in recent years.) In that class, the professor assigned us an essay by Robin Kelley. Published in *Boston Review*, "Black Study, Black Struggle" brings together Kelley's scholarship and experience in Black radical movements to offer advice to contemporary student activists: the demand has its limits, so be careful what you ask for. Writing in response to the 2015 student movements, Kelley observes their tendency to focus on "making the university more hospitable for black students" by asking for things like better DEI initiatives or more representation among faculty. While he agrees that such asks are important, they also proceed from a flawed idea: that the university is capable of being perfected. In truth, he writes, "[the] fully racialized social and epistemological architecture upon which the modern university is built" goes too deep for it to be solved by simply adding more Black and brown faces.

I remember being slightly annoyed that I hadn't encountered these ideas earlier in the term. We'd spent a semester dissecting the problems of our profession, and now here were several thousand words by somebody much smarter than me saying *you can't actually fix it and why would you want to?* (Its capacity to provoke this uncomfortable, galvanizing tension is probably exactly why it was assigned near the end of the semester.) Later, when I formed the reading group, I asked people to read it before our first session. I wanted it there as a kind of mission statement, in case people thought my MO was to make the law school "better." There was an uglier tacit reminder in it, too—that here we were, a roomful of people ready to talk about systemic oppression, but also prepared to set sail into a profession we knew was complicit.

Kelley's critique walks a thin line. As he advises students not to ground their protest in the rhetoric of personal trauma, he necessarily speaks some of the same language—of triggers, trauma, and safe spaces—that is too often used in reactionary takedowns of student activism. But he's careful enough, and sufficiently aware of being embedded in the university himself, that his critique reads as a kind of care. What I appreciate about his essay, every time I read it, is how it gently redirects the focus away from reform, reminding students that it's not their job to improve a broken system. To me, it reads as such a generous, freeing dilation. I think about it every time a white person announces how passionately they want to fix whatever circle of capitalist hell we happen to be stuck in together and then looks at me like, *you too, right?*

I thought about Kelley's essay again during the wave of group statements that flooded the internet in the wake of corporate apologies. As industries vowed to do better by their Black and racialized members, those members issued statements demanding betterment of the worlds that had failed them. A coalition of over one thousand culture workers, including such marquee names as Ava DuVernay, Saidiya Hartman, and Thandiwe Newton, issued five demands as the Black Artists for Freedom. They called on multiple culture industries to divest from policing and give Black artists better material support. The Canadian Association of Black Journalists and the Canadian Journalists of Colour issued seven calls to action to ameliorate the whiteness of our newsrooms, which had produced racist coverage from some of the country's foremost media outlets. In the United States, a collective of Black stage performers served their industry with a twenty-nine-page "new social contract" under the knowing title of "We See You, White American Theater"—turning a handwringing white liberal response into the threat of surveillance. No matter the industry, there were the dissidents, showing up to list their demands.

Though these statements usually had specific and actionable goals, they didn't always. At times, some of them could risk feeling as toothless as the corporate mea culpas they responded to. Part of this blandness is because of how many people they spoke for. When you're drafting a message on behalf of the largest possible group, it's impossible to avoid diffusion. You want something easy to agree with and buzzy to circulate. But too many cooks can dilute the language: the last two demands by the Black Artists for Freedom are for people to "Get Educated" and "Imagine Black Freedom," both of which feel too vague to even qualify as a demand. It makes sense that this happened in a statement meant to speak for a thousand people working across different sectors, each with its own problems and needs.

Aside from watered-down messaging, these calls could also risk feeling insipid because of the sheer number of them floating around at once. I understand that people are bad at seeing patterns of invisible violence when they don't live it daily. I understand, too, the impulse to capitalize on new public awareness and draw a clean line between state violence and something like stage shows. But it felt surprising, even disorienting, that swirling alongside various other bits of data clamoring for our attention—guides for safe protesting, antiracist reading lists, bail-fund requests, Instagram slideshows— were letters that registered group discontent. There's nothing *wrong* with expressing discontent. It's a crucial step and, depending on the movement, specific action isn't even always the goal. But in that particular moment, as both the opening and closing gambit, it seemed to interpret political momentum as a resource at risk of depleting rather than one that requires tending to replenish itself.

In *How to Do Nothing*, Jenny Odell describes how the attention economy offers us information without context. It runs on simplified emotional reactions to quick hits of content—the mechanism of a social media feed. We cannot properly engage with the information we're getting, Odell argues, because the pace and presentation make it impossible to understand how it all relates. A major axis of this "context collapse" is time. Because everything on social media happens instantaneously, it's not the ideal place to engage with content we might need a beat to digest. When it comes to social justice messaging, it helps to know the historical context—or, more basically, just to have time to sit with it and reflect. It's easy to repost a graphic; it's harder to translate that into understanding or action. The collective statements were subject to the same flattening. None of these problems were new, but if you were encountering them for the first time through the Twitter-feed woodchipper, you might be forgiven for thinking so. If you were a CEO feeling guilty for creating a racist office culture that failed your employees, you might *feel* forgiven by refreshing the feed and making the critique go away.

THE SENSE OF exuberant, forceful speech spans the political spectrum and has spawned new life in a different genre: the open letter. Unlike the list of demands, the open letter is not about attaining specific ends, nor is it keyed to leftist politics—if anything, the form, and its adulation of free speech, has come to signify the opposite. But the phrase *open letter* is still used more casually, too. These days, it often gets appended to garden-variety opinion pieces, as if to inject the little thrill of reading someone else's correspondence. Sometimes a letter is "open" because it's in the public interest, like urging people to get vaccinated against COVID-19 or raising awareness about a recent injustice. At others, an open letter is just a way to show you're especially pissed off and don't care who else knows it, like a letter to the premier of Ontario to tell him his "handling of the whole pandemic is a joke" (hard agree).

I should clarify what I'm using the term *open letter* to mean: not just a letter that gets read by more people than the intended recipient, but one that uses *letter* more facetiously. They don't always have an addressee and they don't often expect an answer. They're more like a cry into the void, but borrowing the open-letter title is a way to seem reasonable, like what they really want is to talk. The phrase *open letter* now carries a certain first-amendment frisson, partly owing to a recent, infamous example published in *Harper's Magazine* in 2020: "A Letter on Justice and Open Debate." The *Harper's* letter fits neatly into that most contemporary of genres: a protest against the idea that harmful speech might have consequences. While uprisings for racial justice have been great and all, the letter says, "this needed reckoning has also intensified a new set of moral attitudes and political commitments that tend to weaken our norms of open debate and toleration of differences in favor of ideological conformity." Backlash was swift, as the authors and publishers intended it to be. The letter was signed by powerful characters including Margaret Atwood, Salman Rushdie, Malcolm Gladwell, and, surprisingly, at least one person who also showed up on the "Black Artists for Freedom" list of signatories (who must, one imagines, initial anything that lands in their inbox without reading it carefully). It was also signed by a high number of public figures known for being vocally transphobic. Those cameos inflected the stated desire for uncensored speech with a very different meaning. People who'd endorsed the letter were horrified, upon publication, to see the list of names in full. Some of the signatories even apologized.

Historically, conservative responses to the demand have involved an exaggerated sense of victimization. Think of Nixon's committee; the resources it poured into explicit and ham-fisted calls for violence. We still have those, too—they get published in legacy papers in the form of op-eds—but the sneaky modern update dresses the call to arms in gauzier clothing. The reasons for upholding the old hierarchies are the same—the threat to democracy, the dangerous hostility toward opposing views, the desire to protect the diversity of ideas— but the form has changed. Now, opponents of the demand pretend to affirm the calls for justice, but wonder aloud why it isn't acceptable to disagree with them. They pose a world of edgy hypotheticals— *sure, justice is great, but what if we were allowed to use our platforms to endanger people with impunity?*—and cry censorship when their ideating is criticized for real-world devastation. The open letter registers grievance but stops there, making no effort to imagine the world as it might otherwise be. It name-checks debate but balks at the idea of follow-through. But, in the realm of the demand, there are no true hypothet- icals. You can't fantasize about violence while also disclaiming the desire to bring that violence into being. The point is for the words to make something happen. There is no such thing as *just saying*.

In a world that's wired for instantaneous responses, it makes sense that publicly airing your grievances would seem like the way to engage with a cultural moment, no matter your politics. The de- mand, by contrast, takes time and care; it asks for commitment, but the commitment it requires from the asker is even greater. The de- mand needs *people*. It needs bodies that are willing to come together and throw their weight behind an imagined result. To camp out in the quad, interrupt the ceremony, chant over the organist. Put your body on the line. This is hard and unforgiving work. It's far easier to sign your name to something that lands in your inbox without read- ing it—an apology, an opinion, a fit of pique—and cite that docu- ment as a key contribution to the discourse of the day.

The demand is not a mandatory DEI session or a request to make a toxic, profit-driven practice more hospitable. It's continuing to chant even as capitalism is banging down the door. It's a sudden shift in verbs from *we think* to *we want*.

Do You Read Me

The failure of progressive change in contemporary book publishing is so total that there is now a whole string of books about the failure of progressive change in contemporary book publishing, often backed enthusiastically by big corporate publishers, in an elaborate circuit of denial and absolution. In June 2021, Atria Books released *The Other Black Girl*, by debut novelist Zakiya Dalila Harris. (The book you're reading right now is also published by an Atria imprint.) Harris, a former assistant editor at Knopf, had crafted a novel that dissects the book world's whiteness with an insider's long pent-up precision: Nella, the only Black employee at a storied New York publishing house (similar to Harris's own situation), struggles with the toxic atmosphere of an all-white workplace. On top of that, she has to endure the field's other entry-level burdens, like relentless grunt work and low pay. When Wagner Books finally hires another Black girl, Nella thinks she might have an ally until she starts getting gaslit by the new hire, who seems eerily indulgent of their white bosses' worst impulses. A year and a half before the novel's release, *Publishers Weekly* reported a fourteen-way bidding war between houses that culminated in a seven-figure deal.

The note at the front of the advance copy gives a taste of the enthusiasm that thrummed around the book. The winning bidder "chased it alongside every single editor in town," the note says; "We all wanted this razor-sharp send-up of the starkly white world of book publishing." Acquiring Harris's book was the type of victory that powers a near-obsolete fantasy of the industry: a writer spends years laboring over a manuscript until she is plucked from obscurity by a star-making editor. The editor marshals corporate resources behind a story that's riveting enough to keep readers turning pages (and hopefully send copies flying off the shelves), but that also tells us something essential about the way we live. This is the Jonathan Franzen story, the Jonathan Lethem story, the story of at least one other Jonathan. It is a story that used to involve a lot of handshakes and martinis. It is not a story that usually winds up broadcasting the histories North America prefers not to talk about—but this one did. The old narrative of publishing casts the business as rosy, merit-based, and perfectible. Rather than being driven by the market, it's driven by individual skill, choice, and editors' perceptive responses to artistic genius. It's the one-in-a-million story arc of true love, but also the plotline of bootstrapping capitalist entrepreneurship.

The journey of Harris's novel follows a trajectory that's become increasingly unlikely in the literary world. Because of the book's sharp critique of structural whiteness, its publication also lends heft to a different, feel-good fiction: those from the margins will eventually tilt toward the center by dint of ability, both their own and that of the people in charge. Good white people inherently know the value of diversity and are able to correct literature's historic exclusions one book at a time. Justice à la carte is possible, provided you know how to amplify the right voices.

Harris's novel deserves the hype. It's a sparkling bit of fun, dishing the dirt of the trade in a manner both savage and playful. Scenes of editorial and marketing gaffes made familiar from headlines, like throwing money behind a white-authored book seamed by racist stereotype (with the pressure to "catch it" offloaded onto a racialized junior staff member who's hesitant to piss off the higher-ups), are rendered in the vivid but casual dread of someone who knows, too well, whereof she speaks. Pitched by Harris's agent at the intersection of Jordan Peele's horror film *Get Out* and the catty publishing TV show *Younger*, the book carries sufficient commercial appeal that a hefty offer feels deserved. But laying all that aside for a moment, doesn't it scan as odd that the collective book industry reply to "your working conditions are so racist they're a form of psychological horror" was an ecstatic *yes, drag me*? How hungry do you have to be for expiation—or how constrained your sense of possibility for improvement—to eagerly claim these problems as endemic?

Much of the early press around Harris's deal notes its closeness in time to the *American Dirt* backlash, in which Jeanine Cummins had been paid a reportedly comparable sum to tell a story of Latinx refugees along the Mexico-U.S. border. A few weeks before its release, *American Dirt* attracted a flurry of criticism for its stereotypical depictions of Mexico and of Latinx people. It became the latest flashpoint for issues of representation in publishing—more specifically, it was further evidence that the industry had only partially digested the lesson that representation matters, buying up stories *about* people of color while still overpaying white people to tell them, and arguably not even that accurately. While Latinx writers had been ignored by mainstream houses, *Dirt* was positioned as the definitive novel on immigration in America, a subject that industry lore held to be all but unsellable. The manuscript sailed through executive meetings insulated by a powerful editor, and only when the book hit the outside world, which contained a more realistic cross-section of the reading public than senior-level staff meetings had, did the consequences finally come raining down.

The time, in other words, seemed ripe for a serious reckoning with institutional literary whiteness. There's a subplot in *The Other Black Girl* about a manuscript that basically commits the same sins that *Dirt* was later accused of, told from the perspective of a low-level employee who sees what the all-white senior staff can't. In the novel, Nella is assigned to read and offer notes on one of the house's forthcoming titles, and she agonizes over whether or how to tell her boss that it's cartoonishly racist. The fictional manuscript, which is about the opioid crisis, has only one Black character—"Shartricia"—whose persona is made up exclusively of stereotypes. While telling her boss may be the morally right thing for Nella to do, she hesitates because the white male author is also one of Wagner Books' rainmakers. He's also, no spoilers, incredibly fragile and does not take criticism well. But nobody else clocks the problem. Unless Harris added this subplot in at a later date, its presence indicates these patterns are so baked into the field that she basically predicted *American Dirt* before *American Dirt* happened. More than being a sign of her canniness, it's a sign of an industry that has learned so little that such a situation is more or less mimesis.

In an interview with *Publishers Weekly*, Harris's agent admitted that the *Dirt* fallout came up in early meetings for *The Other Black Girl* and "may have made editors even more confident that [Harris's book] has an audience." The *Dirt* snafu, after all, had been dissected exhaustively by the news cycle. The public seemed keen to know how such a mishap, which looked so obvious in retrospect, could have happened in the first place; deep-dives explored parts of the production process up to a year after the novel came out. This fascination, the *PW* piece implies, may have created an audience hungrier for a book about race, which is a relatively uncommon notion in big publishing. Like the belief that stories about immigration are too unsexy to sell, the warmed-over falsehood that nobody (white) wants to read about race or racism (unless it's a book about slavery) has been used to bar Black writers from the halls of literature for years. The *Dirt* controversy seemed to prove Harris wasn't the only one ready to reckon with the industry's skeletons.

That isn't the only thing the controversy proved. From a business standpoint, the *Dirt* saga has a much happier ending: a tale of executives who read the manuscript, saw dollar signs, and got exactly what they paid for. The book's critical cred may have been shredded, but it still topped the *New York Times* bestseller list and was one of the year's most commercially fruitful titles. And yet the path from one seven-figure acquisition to another—Cummins to Harris—still managed to poke the dormant narrative of improvement; the idea that a switch had been flipped and justice was now flowing in the right direction. But neither *American Dirt* nor *The Other Black Girl* are examples of how to deal with an inequity problem. They're examples of how to deal with a money problem.

THE OTHER BLACK *Girl* isn't airing any dirty laundry that wasn't already extremely public—Harris's innovation is how precisely she documents the issue. Other novels tell a similar story, as do the stats on who gets hired and paid and retained, and whose stories and ideas get put in print. The consensus over publishing's whiteness problem snakes back through the last few years of contemporary fiction, demographic surveys, and digital humanities scholarship. In several recent novels that center millennial life, a character's low-level publishing job functions as a kind of shorthand for both marginality and precarity. As a pattern, it can feel almost uncannily specific. Edie, the narrator of Raven Leilani's incandescent *Luster*, is also one of only two Black people working underpaid staff jobs in a publishing house. Edie's erstwhile double is, like Nella's, more careerist than she is, a Tobagonian woman with an eye on Edie's job and an aptitude for "doing that unthreatening aw-shucks shtick for all the professional whites." Publishing isn't as central to the plot of *Luster* as is it in *The Other Black Girl*, but it has a heavy hand in shaping the harrowing material conditions of Edie's life. Leilani is alert to how life under capitalism is represented in fiction. "I personally need to know how characters eat and pay rent," she said in an interview with *Lux* magazine. These financials, she added, "often have enormous bearing on life's trajectory and plot." In crafting the trajectory and plot of *Luster*, she gave Edie the same job she herself had—an entry-level publishing gig. In New York City, Edie's efforts to survive on that salary involve living in a cockroach-infested apartment and licking tuna from cans. (The paucity of the pay, especially for entry-level jobs, is another thing the industry has spent many years agreeing is a problem while the problem has largely stayed the same.)

The professional setting, and its regressive racial politics, also offers a window into the kinds of stories about Black people that the industry tends to favor. Scanning a pile of books marked for giveaway in the company lobby, Edie reels off a list that plots the coordinates of Blackness in the literary imagination: three slave narratives, one of them about "a tragic mulatto who raises the dead with her magic chitlin pies"; a "domestic drama about a black maid"; and an "'urban' romance where everybody dies by gang violence." The only book description with any information about its author is "a book about a Cantonese restaurant, which may or may not have been written by a white woman from Utah, whose descriptions of her characters rely primarily on rice-based foods." It's a dismal list any way you slice it, but what's notable is the lack of detail about the authors' backgrounds other than the final example. That only one author gets (potentially) identified leaves open the chance that the other books, built on tired caricatures of Blackness, were either written by white people or were the only stories by Black writers the white-staffed imprint was willing to gamble on. As the books sit there abandoned in the lobby, demoted to the status of "Diversity Giveaway[s]," that gamble doesn't seem to have paid off.

Ling Ma's 2017 debut, *Severance*, is a novel about the mindless repetition of office work that presciently rendered a pandemic a few years before COVID-19. In *Severance*, Ma appoints publishing as the chief representative of empty capitalist labor. Candace Chen, the daughter of Chinese immigrants, has spent five years working dutifully (if disaffectedly) at Spectra, a New York–based publishing house, coordinating the production of specialty Bibles. Candace is good enough at her job—she sits down at her desk, the hours disappear, and the tasks get done—but her heart's not in it. A photographer outside work hours, Candace aspires to design coffee-table books alongside the company's "Art Girls"—a group of "colt-legged, flaxen-haired" women in their twenties, who tote "discounted Miu Miu and Prada" as they swan along the office hallways. When a spore-based disease blossoms into a global crisis, Candace accepts a lucrative contract to stay in the office after Spectra's executives have fled New York, coordinating Bible production with the company's flagging business partners in Hong Kong. In both the city and the world around her, the numbers of infected people skyrocket, with victims trapped in an endless loop of unthinking repetition—a family droning grace over a rotted meal, an elderly neighbor fumbling with the keys outside her apartment. Candace doesn't cling to her comparably numbing job amid global catastrophe because she has an unusually passionate desire to be one of those art-world white girls, but because her work routines anchor her to the only stability she has left. Candace's job, like Edie's and Nella's, taps a vein of interrelated contemporary problems. Want to tell a story about the abject horrors of surviving under racial capitalism in a world blanched by homogeneity? Give your character an entry-level publishing job.

Whiteness, precarity, tokenized hiring—these literary tropes form their own consensus about how inhospitable the industry can be, especially for junior-level workers who are neither white nor wealthy. There are entire savage meme accounts dedicated to driving this point home on Instagram. These novels concur with *The Other Black Girl* and the New York editors who bid on it: yes, the situation is really bad.

Moreover, publishing has incorporated the story of its flaws back into itself to be repackaged as product (this book, I suppose, included). The absorption of dissent isn't surprising; loosening the valve to release a little built-up tension is a time-honored tactic that lets the status quo carry on unchecked. Publishing is a business like any other, and especially at the big commercial houses, decisions are made in the service of the bottom line. At the same time, what makes the lack of demographic change more disheartening—and the cannibalization of critique seem darker—is the amount of breath the industry has spent on professing how much it wants to do better.

Because the numbers tell a different story. In 2019, independent publisher Lee & Low Books released its second Diversity Baseline Survey. The results, widely circulated in news and social media, showed negligible improvement over the inaugural survey four years prior. Measuring the race, gender, orientation, and ability of workers across department and seniority, the survey put figures to a problem that was already long known. The results reported an overall 76 percent of white employees—three percentage points lower than the outcome of the 2015 survey, which wasn't considered statistically significant, especially since the 2019 survey had had a bigger sample size. (For reference, the population of white people in the United States, the most recent census reports, is 60.1 percent.) The percentage of white employees fluctuated slightly depending on the position: the highest concentration, at 85 percent, was clustered in editorial; the lowest, at 51 percent, was among the interns. The percentage of Black workers hovered at a relatively stable 3–5 percent across all of the categories with exceptions in the intern and editorial pools—8 percent and 1 percent, respectively. Though the decision to acquire a book engages multiple departments and requires buy-in from far more than one person, when it comes to the laps that manuscript submissions land in and who picks the ones that go forward, editors are the frontline.

These numbers were released during the long winter of *American Dirt* but still a few weeks prior to *The Other Black Girl*'s deal announcement, perhaps stoking the latter's fire even hotter. The results also came out before the uprisings against police violence sent corporate hand-wringing into an even higher gear. The pattern established across industries—where CEOs issued statements in support of Black lives, calling forth an immediate surfeit of evidence to the contrary—seemed to take place with particular verve in the publishing space. Each of the Big Five publishers made the requisite post, though the message took a different form depending on who issued it: white text on a black square; letters containing fleshed-out accountability plans; or an antiracist booklist-cum-shopping list appended to a statement. But, at the same time as they issued these pledges to justice, some presses doubled down on practices that indicated the opposite. With towering barricades around any port of entry, the book industry has always been complicit in marginalization. More recently, it has increased its stock in injustice by continuing to publish material that threatens or harms the lives of the people the profession already shuts out. Books about the Trump presidency were incredible sellers. As material by or about white supremacists grew more lucrative, the gap between the word ("we stand with you," "we're listening") and the action (". . . but we're also giving a million dollars to someone who believes your existence is worthless/deserving of extermination/up for debate") pushed the theater of good intentions beyond credulity.

Before and even during the wave of statements and action plans, the book industry got away with a lot: using AI to trawl the text of classic novels for nominally raceless characters, then deciding Frankenstein (or whomever) was actually Black and issuing a series of special editions right in time for February—as Barnes & Noble did for their swiftly revoked "Diverse Editions" initiative. Paying bottom dollar for racialized writers' books (if they bought their books at all) but throwing money at white ones to tell the same story riddled with inaccuracies. Keeping certain acquisitions secret from a company's staff and then announcing a marquee title by a fascist-adjacent public intellectual, or alleged child molester, or murderous cop, in a surprise blitz. This dissonance persists because publishers are trying to have it two different ways: to claim moral progress by anointing a few more marginalized writers than it has in the past, while disavowing the language of progress or justice altogether when they give a platform to hate speech (at that point, it becomes an issue of free expression). But neither of these frameworks tell a complete story—the most relevant metric is what's considered sellable.

WHEN THE HASHTAG #PublishingPaidMe tore across Twitter, it exposed glaring disparities in the size of book advances between Black and non-Black authors. (Other inequities became apparent, too, like the fact that men tended to get higher advances, especially if they were white.) As more writers sounded off about their paydays, a trend emerged: Publishing houses seemed generally content to throw six-figure sums at white authors with unproven track records—in one case, six figures to a white woman who'd written a viral *New York Times* essay but had not published previous books—while Black writers, including Jesmyn Ward, received much lower sums despite having award-winning titles to their name. The anecdote that Ward shared was especially chilling: she and her agent had to agitate for her advance to break six figures even after she'd won a National Book Award for fiction (her first of two). A book's advance is determined in part by the projected size of its audience—so someone who's won a major literary award is likelier to come with a built-in readership, and therefore be a safer financial bet, than someone with handful of Twitter followers and a topical proposal—but once race was factored into the equation, the calculus got messier.

The financial imbalances of #PublishingPaidMe were driven by a set of outdated and racist beliefs: That books by and about Black and racialized people did not have sufficient commercial appeal to merit a big advance. That whiteness is the mouthpiece for universal storytelling. That—as many Black writers and publishing staffers have reported hearing white people say in meetings—Black people don't read or buy books. At the same time as these conversations about advances sparked and spread, the sales figures seemed to give the lie to the premise: Of *course* there was an audience for Black writing. Black writers' books were climbing the bestseller charts as well-meaning people ran to assemble their antiracist reading lists. This eagerness on the part of the audience, in turn, stoked fresh incentive for presses to gobble up acquisitions from Black writers. (This was around the time that I sold my book.) But it would be wrong to read this fresh enthusiasm as signifying a sea change. Mainstream houses have a reliably circular interest in Black writing. As Kaitlyn Greenidge writes in *VQR*, this sort of nominal renaissance rotates back around every couple of decades, when "publishing gets very excited about the trend of black people writing fiction" and treats every time as though it's the first. More recently, such periods are likely to correlate with a highly visible incident of police brutality, when the violence that haunts the lives of so-called "niche" voices is shunted into public view too spectacularly to ignore or deny. Caught in the floodlight, a roomful of white decision-makers freeze and demand of one another: How many of the people on our list are Black?

Part of the reason it's been so hard to shift this outdated target of what "sells" is because the conditions that created it haven't changed, either. The same inequities have riven the book industry for decades. Entry-level salaries have stayed famously low while the major employers cluster in America's priciest city, as if the people who get in should consider themselves lucky to be there and not ask questions (questions like *can I get a raise so I don't have to lick tuna from a can?*). The people who had the resources to get there in the first place—white people, mostly—are insulated at the top, as junior staffers struggle many rungs beneath them. The field's most visible port of entry—the internship—historically pays nothing at all, restricting the candidate pool to those with inherited wealth or other financial safety nets. (This is slowly beginning to change, with some publishers now funding their internship programs.) Snagging an entry-level spot is also famously competitive. In "The Unbearable Whiteness of Publishing," James Ledbetter's two-part *Village Voice* feature from 1995, a former Norton editor confesses that he's never had to take out a job ad to replace a departing editorial assistant: "I lift my pinky and the most staggering résumés hit my desk. They come from a network of agents, writers, and academics . . . [the process is] not closed consciously, but it doesn't seem to have to open." This doesn't just speak to the field's competitiveness, but its insularity. Professional networks also play a role in how whiteness keeps respawning. To enter the halls of literature, you almost always have to know a guy.

"The Unbearable Whiteness of Publishing" appeared almost three decades ago. Twenty-six years later, the pace of change had proved so glacial that *Publishers Weekly* ran a redux that concluded nothing much had changed in the interim. Co-authored by Shelly Romero and Adriana M. Martínez Figueroa, both of whom work in the industry, the piece traces bright lines between Ledbetter's grim picture and the modern realities of book publishing: the prohibitive costs of academic programs, the prevalence of nepotism, the inadequate wages, the tokenized hiring, the absence of minoritized people in decision-making positions, and the lack of advancement. Where Romero and Figueroa depart from Ledbetter, though, is in citing recent efforts that have begun to chip away at the historical monolith. In the past few years, there have been numerous senior-level hires of Black and racialized editors and executives across presses. New imprints have bloomed, like Phoebe Robinson's Tiny Reparations (Dutton/Plume), Legacy Lit (Hachette), and Joy Revolution (Random House Children's Books), headed up by minoritized editors and writers and with the mandate to acquire and nurture work by writers of color. Across the industry, there's been an effort to let down a drawbridge or two by inviting manuscripts submitted by writers without literary agents, or offering paid fellowship opportunities to people who weren't streamed straight from a publishing program, or conceding to pay interns. In the spring of 2021, Roxane Gay announced her own imprint at Grove Atlantic, Roxane Gay Books, which will focus on work by writers from underrepresented communities. Among the imprint's various methods for nudging open publishing's doors—accepting unagented submissions, offering a "crash course" in the business to people who lack access to traditional inroads—is its commitment to minimum advances. As #PublishingPaidMe showed, the extreme discretion in offering advances can breed inequity. (Gay has been open about the smallness of her advance for *Bad Feminist*, a fact she tweeted was "pretty well known" even before the #PublishingPaidMe discourse.)

Hopefully, these initiatives will make a dent in the industry's homogeneity. But they're still operating within an environment driven by the profit motive, an impulse that shapes the books that get signed and the institutional support they attract. When it comes to marketability, Zora Neale Hurston has had the industry's number since 1950. Her essay "What White Publishers Won't Print," which originally appeared in the *Negro Digest*, gives a blunt assessment of the trade as "in business to make money." This priority, in turn, makes it inherently averse to stories about minoritized people. Publishers cater to the imagination of the white American reader and disseminate texts that milk their preconceptions—like the idea that Black people, Indigenous peoples, and other minoritized communities are flat stereotypes incapable of complex inner lives. To offer those white readers a story of the "higher emotions and love life" of racialized people that lacked the requisite "racial tension" would piss them off, run afoul of the moneymaking motive, and therefore be a bad call. Hurston's vision of publishing's circuitry, brutal as it is, doesn't buy the idea that improvement is possible. It's not that publishers don't feel for the plight of the disenfranchised, she says; it's that they're not in the business of feeling, as feeling is bad business. Nor are they in the business of educating, or campaigning for justice: "Sympathetic as [publishers] might be," she writes, "they cannot afford to be crusaders." Seventy-plus years later, while Hurston's thesis still feels very true, corporate behemoths seem to be wrestling with that statement. They cannot *afford* to be crusaders, but becoming a crusader is also a newly topical and attractive proposition.

How much you buy Hurston's assessment depends on how accountable you imagine publishers ought to be for the material they put out. For a Black writer in 1950, who witnessed firsthand how difficult it was for her peers to make it into print, Hurston's cynical calculus—that ethical profit is impossible so why try—makes sense. As big publishers consolidate into fewer entities, her diagnosis only seems more prescient. But the profit motive cuts awkwardly across publishing's other, nobler priority—the implied duty to be, in the words of mystery writer Walter Mosley, "the benefactor of the First Amendment." At the risk of stating the obvious, being the arbiter of what gets printed and circulated is impossible to untangle from politics, even when—as often seems to be the case—publishers try to pretend it's not. But while Hurston's thesis still holds, a different set of expectations are being put forth as staffers, readers, and writers demand that book behemoths show more social responsibility. While dedicated imprints and splashy acquisitions and senior-level appointments go some way toward redressing past wrongs, they don't address the field's deeper priorities—*why* a publisher elevates the work it does, who profits from it, and who might be harmed by it.

THE GULF BETWEEN the nobility of the profession and the unseemly race for profitability finds a surprising advocate in the final season of *Younger*, a TV show that's spent six years ignoring the book bubble's unsavory aspects (apart from, I think accidentally, its whiteness). Liza Miller, a plucky Gen-X white lady, outwitted a different brand of discriminatory hiring in season one by pretending to be a millennial. Later, she rises swiftly through the ranks as white women of any generation get to do, taking naturally to a life of industry glitz. But by the show's final season, most of the sexiness seems like it's been titrated out of the job. The publishing house's buzzy young imprint, Millennial Press, has been integrated into its stuffier parent company by board decree. Charles Brooks, the publisher, spends most scenes agonizing over the company coffers and raising his brooding eyebrows whenever his staffers want to offer a high advance. At pitch meetings, book proposals are assessed solely for their blockbuster potential, whether the property on offer is a climate change manifesto authored by a Greta Thunberg caricature (whose book would probably sell because of the size of her built-in platform) or the memoirs of a sex-obsessed surfer (whose book would probably sell because of his abs on the cover). Before she sleeps with the surfer, whose book she's also tipped to edit, Liza listens as he waxes about how he gets to spend his days doing the thing he loves. Sounding slightly bewildered, Liza agrees that, yes, she does, too—though the preceding office scenes full of brutal, capitalistic decision-making have made that easy for both her and the viewer to forget. Part of what made *Younger* such frothy fun is that it explored an elite, cloistered world without ever being burdened by realism—especially when it came to money, an invisible tide that had, by season seven, lifted the main cast into casual affluence and property ownership. All of this made it especially surprising when the show pivoted to a sudden portrayal of publishing's mercenary streak.

But the diagnosis put forth by an individual television show—or gossipy industry novel, or exasperated op-ed, or even the static data of a single-year demographic survey—only gives a limited glimpse into the extent of the problem. Recent work in the digital humanities crunches the consensus of creeping dread into hard numbers, studying it at a scale only made possible by computational methods. Studies like Richard Jean So's perpetually startling *Redlining Culture: A Data History of Racial Inequality and Postwar Fiction* put facts and figures to a thing people knew to be true but didn't have the words—or numbers—to articulate. So's book introduces the concept of *cultural redlining*, a term he uses to describe the patterns of racial exclusion in the U.S. literary industries. Exploring the output of one big publisher, Random House, from 1950 to 2000, So tracks inequality across the production (editing), reception (reviewing), distinction (awards and sales), and canonization (scholarship) stages. What he finds is alarming: During this fifty-year period, 97 percent of novels Random House published were by white writers, with Black writers accounting for a mere 2 percent. Even worse is the stability of that statistic over time. There's a blip in the 1970s that So isolates as, dismally, the "Toni Morrison effect"—an uptick in Black-authored novels that aligns with the years Toni Morrison worked at Random House as an editor, acquiring titles by writers like Gayl Jones and Toni Cade Bambara. (One other tiny rise takes place in the 1950s around the time of Ralph Ellison's *Invisible Man*—recall Kaitlyn Greenidge's diagnosis that every few years "publishing gets very excited about the trend of black people writing fiction.") But after Morrison left, the line slunk back down into flatness, where it lay, detumescent, until the end of the millennium.

The books' contents reflect similar patterns of segregation. Studying the most popular words that white writers use to describe white characters, So finds that literary-fiction writers, at least at Random House across those fifty years, are "self-fixated . . . on their own racial identity as refracted through their work identity. If a white person shows up in their novel, he or she is likely to be some kind of novelist or literary person." By contrast, when it comes to how writers describe their Black characters, there's a dearth of what So calls, rather diplomatically, "semantic variance." Writers fall back on the same careful and anodyne words, like *fellow*, again and again, expressing the familiar hesitance of a white person not sure which of the words for Black people they're allowed to say. Hurston warned us about this seventy years ago. Data like this is dismaying but it's also delightfully impossible to argue with, rendering moot any hint of conspiratorial or self-satisfied thinking. Publishing houses say they have a history of investing in Black writers? Point to the numbers. Literary scholars advance the story that multicultural writing is supplanting the old systemic exclusions? Ditto. A white male writer publishes an essay bemoaning the pain of reverse marginalization? Buddy!

Analyses of more recent years have extended the same flat line. A data-driven article in *Public Books*, "Who Gets to Be a Writer?" finds that 90 percent of the books published since 2000 have been by white writers, even as racialized authors have become statistically more likely to win a literary prize than they are to get published in the first place. The latter depends more on the discretion of an awards committee than the profit-driven acquisition process, so it isn't exactly proof of progress. But what matters *more* than race, the authors continue, "is where a writer went to college or university." When you factor race into those findings, things move even further away from a cozy story of improvement. Sure, a Black student who graduated from Harvard is many times more likely to win a literary prize than someone who is not a Harvard grad, but getting to Harvard at all means clearing a whole other series of hurdles that are set up to favor whiteness. It's not that being racialized gets you literary accolades (ha!), it's that attending an elite school boosts your chances.

Laura B. McGrath examined how discrimination warps a different part of the publication process, the comp title, in the *Los Angeles Review of Books*. Comp titles (short for *comparable* or *comparative*) try to predict a book's performance by projecting it against the sales of similar, already-published titles. A manuscript's expected success is one factor in an editor's choice whether or not to buy it or how much to spend. The guiding logic of comps, McGrath explains, is *"if it worked before, it will work again."* Prioritizing the sure bets "[creates] a rigid process of acquisition without much room for individual choice or advocacy." The relevant factor is what possible future books are being compared *to*. Studying publishers' catalogues from 2013 to 2019, McGrath found that of the top 500 books that were routinely cited as comps, 478 of them had been written by white people. Since there's a high probability that any given submission is being held up against books by white authors, there is also a high risk a title will be disqualified if it departs too much from them. The process, like other parts of the industry, naturally favors whiteness. Considering this procedure, it's easier to see how the disparities in #PublishingPaidMe may have happened. An editor might agree to bid on a book by a Black writer, but if that book doesn't look sufficiently similar to the guiding list of lucrative books by white writers, then perhaps it's worth spending less on.

The book industry's business model drives these statistics. The postwar period kicked off a now-familiar cycle of buyouts and mergers that's never really ended, shaving down the list of places that control more of the market's literary content. By the late 1990s, six book publishers controlled between 60 and 80 percent of the American book market. Now, we're down to five big publishers, who are still trying to consolidate further: in November 2020, the parent company of Penguin Random House went public with its intent to buy Simon & Schuster. The proposed entity would have a disproportionately large influence over the books published in the United States. A year later, in November 2021, the United States Department of Justice sued to block the sale, arguing that it "would result in substantial harm to authors." Like selling a novel about the failures of publishing, conglomeration is a way to absorb and neutralize threat. It also exerts a major homogenizing force on literary output. While the prewar era saw presses mostly "committed to aesthetic evaluation without strong regard for the bottom line," writes Richard Jean So, once they started consolidating, "the new era's watchword was 'the bestseller.'" Books were judged less as intellectual projects and more as commercial products.

In this context, there are even fewer channels by which a writer or editor, from a group shunted to the industry's margins, might hope to make inroads. (This, in turn, allowed nonprofit presses, like Graywolf Press, Coffee House Press, and Milkweed Editions, to define themselves in opposition by trumpeting diversity as their mission. This decision, Dan Sinykin and Edwin Roland argue, was made "less out of principle than convenience," as such priorities were attractive to donors and funding bodies.) In a keynote address at the 1981 American Writers' Congress, Toni Morrison—herself a hire with an outsized, if implicit, responsibility to help fix her employer's demographic stats—railed against what the changing business model meant for books and the people who write and edit them. "Writers today are regarded as toys," Morrison said. "Editors are now judged by the profitability of what they acquired rather than by what they acquire . . . We are in an adversary relationship with publishers."

IN THE LONG, halting process of slouching toward equity, certain premises are easy to implement: Representation matters. Hire more diverse people. To put these ideas into practice can look like the start of reform. But too often, such efforts are treated as ends rather than first steps, leaving an even bigger mess in their wake. *Representation matters* got co-opted into a referendum on white writers' license to imagine: *But why can't the story be written by someone who's a different [insert some axis of identity here] from the characters?* white people asked, while books by those same writers kept getting denied dollars and attention. *Hire more diverse people* has proved somewhat more actionable—in addition to bringing on senior-level personnel, a number of publishing houses have vowed to self-report their demographics and have buffed up their strategic plans to attract and retain minoritized talent.

At the same time, increasing the "diversity of voices" in the room doesn't suddenly signal a commitment to dismantling anti-Blackness and structural discrimination. First, it puts a tacit (and sometimes explicit) pressure on the new hires to correct for the rest of the company's sins. I have no doubt that the editors of new imprints are committed to improving their industry's track record—and they're doing urgent work. But I also hope they get the internal support that they need to fully execute their vision; without it, they'll just be like Nella in *The Other Black Girl* but with a better paycheck. But there's another way we've seen *diversity* get co-opted. Close on the heels of the statements supporting Black lives—so close it was dizzying— were a series of book deals with right-wing political personalities, including former members of the Trump administration, who have done a lot to prove how little they think Black and minoritized lives matter. While it's been a longstanding practice for publishers to acquire books across the political spectrum, these deals, in the wake of social unrest and corporate apology, looked like walking back what had been promised only a few months before. As ever, it was about making the smart financial choice. Books about polarizing political figures have historically been good bets, and the warp-speed catastrophes of the Trump presidency offered endless juicy angles—memoirs, tell-alls, exposés. Michael Wolff's *Fire and Fury* and Bob Woodward's *Fear* have sold millions of copies, and the audience appetite showed no signs of slowing. During a pandemic and an economic crisis, this was a huge boon. In that situation, a behemoth corporation literally can't afford to be a crusader.

But it's also really awkward if you've just circulated a statement saying that you promise to become a crusader; that you "stand against racism and violence . . . now and always." Workers within publishing, and people across social media, pointed out how virulently hypocritical this was. The answer, from executives, was often to call on the language of diversity—the diversity of ideas—as Justice Powell smiled down upon them. Recasting the books as part of a wider mission to showcase a broader range of voices is a cynical reply, reframing the issue as one of free speech (of the people in power whom these books benefit) rather than basic human rights (of the people, both in and outside of publishing, whom they threaten). Sometimes, the demands to drop the books had tangible effects. Some of the acquisitions, like books by Senator Josh Hawley (who many believe contributed to inciting the Capitol insurrection) and Jonathan Mattingly (one of the cops who broke down the door of Breonna Taylor's home and shot her), were authored by people accused of acts so horrifying and patently undemocratic that executives quickly rescinded their decisions after the backlash. But other calls, like giving a two-book deal to Mike Pence and acquiring a book by Kellyanne Conway, have held firm in the face of protest. The public has proven it has an appetite for Trump-adjacent books, those titles are projected to make a killing, and a behemoth corporation is a massive mouth to feed. These books were bought by Simon & Schuster (which, I feel compelled to disclose one last time, also published this book about institutional hypocrisy), which has been very canny about striking these deals, despite public criticism and protracted employee protest.

Perhaps the principle that's been most badly implemented in all of this is, surprisingly, the truism that diversity—gender and racial diversity—is good for business. The corporate world has been hawking this idea for a long time. With publishing having embraced most of the other best practices for profit, this one seems conspicuously absent. And yet the industry still clings to the veneer of progressivism, a value that's arguably been shunted further from its business model despite more vocal attempts to claim it.

It's possible for the industry to lower its barriers to entry, slowly but steadily rebalancing the resources that have long been concentrated in the hands of wealthy, white New Yorkers. But the central fiction—that the world of books will bend naturally toward every kind of justice—has long since expired. The self-interest of the economic motive curbs the possibilities of the moral one, no matter how good the intentions. When profit is king and hate sells, you're always going to pick the thing that gets you rich.

Dead or Canadian

There were four of us around the table, eating tacos at a Nashville bar, when someone suggested we play "Dead or Canadian." I'd never heard of the game before but the title alone was enough to ping an instinctual dread. The rules of play are basically there in the name—you toss out the monikers of poor creative souls who didn't *make it*, in work or in life, and then everyone guesses which kind of death they met—but I still asked to have it explained to me. When you think you've discovered one of your private horrors is another country's parlor game, it's prudent to double-check. I was a few days into a monthlong trip to the United States. Nashville was a quick stopover on the way to a contract job in New York City, and already I was being put in my place. Still, I bit the bullet and said I was up for it; we were among friends, and bullets are very American. As the only Canadian present I felt a little exposed, but my vulnerability was also my advantage—the competition was an American and two U.K. transplants, one of them my partner, Philip, the only person my sangfroid wasn't fooling.

I didn't feel defensive because of my passport, but because of my vocation. As a person of Canadian persuasion who works in the arts and is currently alive, that punch line is my destiny. Careers like mine are the reason it exists. I can labor my whole life and smash every record and maybe even get myself a green card, but people will still grade me by those two ignoble options. If you're from the United States, the appeal of the game is obvious, a flash of the small-t trump card of cultural dominance against your opponent's weaker hand. For Canadians, it's harder to see the fun. Don't get me wrong, my country deserves to be dragged for any hint of exceptionalism, which it emits so loudly and often that Americans can preemptively recite the talking points. In that sense, the joke is a justified smug tax. But it's also a reminder that Canada's tidy, modest institutions have lowered the ceiling on its creative professions. There's also—and I knew even in the moment, as I said all of this through a mouthful of Baja fish taco, that I was taking it too personally—something very stay-in-your-lane about the presumption that a Canadian artist will never get big enough to be seen as one of them. They'd sooner call you dead. So much for assimilation! I ended my rant by snarling, "Anyway, let's *play*."

As it turns out, my hit rate for issuing accurate death sentences was no better than anyone else's at the table. Despite Canada's best efforts to instill in me a sense of patriotism, something clearly hadn't taken. I possessed no innate wisdom that sparked at the names of my compatriots, felt no special alarm go off when they needed rescuing from imminent demise. Quite the contrary: I accidentally killed a lot of people. Maybe my score was tanking because I was distracted by the terror of stepping on my own grave. Or maybe it was because I, like a good American, have been known to occasionally confuse the Great White North with a kind of cultural death.

I have no metrics for how widespread "Dead or Canadian" is as an American pastime—it comes from a late-1980s game show, *Remote Control*, that had a four-year stint on MTV—but it makes sense to me that the power imbalance is figured, from a U.S. pop-culture standpoint, as a form of play. For people like me, it's an identity crisis. America looms vast in the Canadian artistic imagination. During the developmental stage that involves the ecstatic and indiscriminate consumption of culture, U.S. output forms, purely by numbers, a huge chunk of what young creators grow up nerding out on. By that point, it's passed into your blood. At the same time, you're sub- jected to a diffuse indoctrination program, from education to the law, that implies you're supposed to do something different from what *they* do. You're taught to value art that expresses a distinctly Ca- nadian point of view. You're taught such a thing as a Canadian point of view exists at all and that there's a whole set of aesthetic short- hand to convey it. You feel the expectation, transmitted at varying frequencies—who gets funding, who gets jobs, who gets published, who gets canonized—that your work will also express that short- hand, or define itself in predictable opposition to it. Some of these premises are the growing pains of a still-young country, others are my own paranoia. But I've long understood it as a kind of vise ap- plied to storytelling. It has always struck me as a deeply unfair set of conditions under which to expect anyone to make art, let alone the kind that defines a nation.

If you're lucky enough to eke out a piece of the pie and end up *working* in Canadian cultural industries, you're in for a surprise. In the halls of studios and newsrooms and production offices, a different principle reigns: real success means flying south. "Go to America," veterans will tell their younger colleagues, held in place by property or kids or the more mundane ballasts of habit and time. "Get out while you still can." The prospect of my moving south had been coming up for years, resurfacing across my work in various fields and usually raised by people other than me. As a voice actor, I traveled to LA for awards shows and met with directors who told me, correctly, that I'd never get cast in a blockbuster from all the way up north. As a law student, I was urged to apply to New York firms for better money and job prospects. As a fact-checker and editor floating between contract gigs, my situation mirrored what I heard dispensed as common knowledge: There's not much here.

No matter the context, the southward drag was present and forceful, a density in the atmosphere: *Get out while you still can*. For years, I hadn't listened. I'd heard it so many times I stopped taking it seriously, writing it off as one more thing people just feel entitled to say to you in Canada, like *diversity is our strength* and *but where are you really from?*

Instead, I stayed, because staying was comfortable. I also resented being told by other people to take my life, tear it up, and start again. If the factor limiting my potential was truly just a fluke of birth and borders, the mistake didn't seem like mine to pay for, especially if the price was to uproot my whole existence. Yet, at the same time, I felt the nagging worry these people were right. Their advice set churning the same gut-level dread that later made me overreact to "Dead or Canadian." They must have seen something light up in my eyes when they told me to go. A tiny American inside me, screaming *let me out*.

I've always suspected that my work never fit this place and the image it wants to project. The kinds of things I wanted to write seemed not to exist in Canada; often, Canada sent me that message right back. I could never get my essays published at home, or get the media industry to care about me at all, until I started picking up American bylines. With fiction I was luckier, at least at first; when I walked away from short stories done up in an earnest first-person to start writing stuff I thought was funny, literary journals stopped replying. In a meeting to discuss my roundly rejected novel manuscript I was tickled when a genial book editor, clearly believing he bore bad news, told me over coffee that I wrote with the meanness of an early-aughts white American man. *Yes*, I thought. *Exactly what I was going for.*

The real reason I never leaped at the advice to hightail it out is because I was afraid. My stubbornness didn't bloom from any lack of want but more like an excess of it, desire at a scale I distrusted my ability to control. Or so I told myself, since *wanting it too much* sounds sexier than *crushing fear of failure*. For all of my complaints, I was content to swim in a pond of this exact circumference and nothing more. I praised the people who got out, but wasn't sure I had it in me to be one of them. But that anxiety is also a potent indicator: My most powerful attractions have been threaded with the suspicion that I'm not quite good enough to merit the object of desire. Which may be the most Canadian thing I've ever said.

AT THE TURN of the millennium, Molson Canadian released a commercial meant to inject new verve into both domestic beer sales and national pride. The sixty-second spot, affectionately known as "The Rant," premiered during the 2000 Academy Awards telecast. It opens on a clean-shaven white man in a plaid flannel shirt, striding across an empty stage as shots of the Canadian flag billow on screens behind him. When he reaches the microphone he pauses, gives a half-hearted wave to an unseen audience, and clears his throat—gestures that, along with his overall mien, are clearly meant to scan as polite. "Hey, I'm, uh, I'm not a lumberjack, or a fur trader." His voice is soft, rueful, unsure of his entitlement to take up space. But he's going to do it anyway because he's got a bone to pick: Someone has been talking shit about this guy, and he's here to set things straight. As he recites his grievances, his voice rising in volume and vehemence—"I have a prime minister, not a president. I speak English and French, *not* American"—the other shoe drops. Who would be so cruel as to sully the name of this affable dude who "pronounce[s] it *about*, not *a boot*"? Why, *Americans*, of course. The rant, then, isn't just about national fervor, but reifying differences like "I believe in peacekeeping, not policing; diversity, not assimilation" as proof that Canada is *"the best part of North America"* (by this point, he's full-on yelling). Over the soaring strings of "Land of Hope and Glory" and mounting cheers, the ad reaches its apex: "My name is Joe! And *FUCK AMERICA!!!*"

Just kidding. Come on, politeness is a tenet of Canada 101! The punch line, also the slogan of the ad campaign, is: "And *I AM CANADIAN*." But they aren't Joe's *final* words—he ends his rant with a coquettish "thank you," a self-serving flourish by ad execs panting for the viewer to twig how quintessentially Canadian it is to show gratitude after climaxing. The ad is a crafty little piece of zealotry, making like it wants to dismantle various fictions when it's actually much more interested in codifying them. In doing so, the commercial becomes a vehicle for some of the most pervasive, feel-good myths of Canadian nationalism. Some of them are comparatively benign, like the idea that niceness is part of the national character, or that everyone here speaks fluent English and French, or that Canada's white men would be any likelier to hesitate before bellowing their personal grievances into a microphone. Other fictions require more delusion to believe in: That Canada does not have a racism problem, or an epidemic of police brutality. And, most destructively, that the national reverence for diversity is, like the politeness of its citizens, just *there*, unflappable and eternal. *This is us*, the ad said; *this is who we are*. Which makes it especially disappointing that the identity it paints is largely contentless, a negative that emerges from denial and self-serving oppositions. If we had to come out swinging for our definitive "thing," couldn't we have picked a personality a little less pathetic? Delivered to a dark theater full of anonymous supporters—rather than, say, an American driving his finger into Joe's chest—the speech feels oddly passive, like coming up with your sickest burns in the shower after the real fight's over. Or, perhaps, like building an ego around a magnified crisis that was never really that big to begin with.

Is this the expression of a distinctly Canadian point of view? The creative team behind it certainly thought so, as did a lot of the country. The ad spot's creative lead, Glen Hunt, told the *Globe and Mail* that he drew on years of work in New York City, in which his American friends would torment him with the stereotypes that later appeared in the commercial. He sure showed them! The Molson team expanded the list of misconceptions through extensive focus groups, during which they also found inspiration for Joe's delivery. When they asked people what it means to be Canadian, the *Globe* piece relays, "[m]any would start off slowly . . . but by the end of the interview they had worked themselves up emotionally." They didn't come out and *say* most of the people in the focus groups were white, but they didn't have to. Can you imagine what the list of responses to *what does Canada mean to you?* would have looked like if they'd asked Indigenous people? If immigrants had had the chance to answer *what are some of the ways you find yourself getting stereotyped?* Fueled by personal resentment and the repressed passion of its target consumers, the ad fanned the flames of a national obsession and maple leaf–pilled a nation.

When "The Rant" aired in cinemas and bars, people would get on their feet and cheer. Joe Canadian—the character's full name, in all its ethnic and imaginative richness—would do the monologue as part of the halftime show at hockey games. Politicians, including the former Conservative Prime Minister Joe Clark, would reference it in speeches, presumably as proof of being down with the culture. Then–heritage minister Sheila Copps even played the commercial for an American crowd at the International Press Institute World Congress, as proof of what, I'm not sure. Canucks felt *seen*. The spot wasn't without its critics—some people thought its brand of rah-rah nationalism made us look *more* like the United States; others, like Ontario's former minister of consumer affairs, thought it was a sign of insecurity (it was) that was so rude to our neighbors, it tarnished the Canadian brand (it didn't). But it was a big win for Molson, whose market share in English Canada rose by 2.5 percent, or around $50 million, the next year. It was also a big win for Jeff Douglas, the actor who played Joe—so big, in fact, that he decided to capitalize on this new professional momentum by moving to LA.

Can you tell this is my favorite part of the story? Canadians *lost their shit*. Joe was a national treasure, an icon of cultural pride, and in a country notoriously short on those kinds of rallying points— which was basically the thesis of the Molson spot—too precious to lose. (But also: Maybe this is what you get for staking your sense of self on a beer ad?) The *National Post*, a right-leaning newspaper, launched an unauthorized job hunt on Douglas's behalf. They called on Canadian film and TV executives to offer him a gig so plum, he couldn't refuse. Allegedly, the best they could come up with was a guest-starring role, an anecdote so demonstrative of the problem it approaches parable. "His name was Joe, and he was Canadian," began a *Washington Post* item, scenting the funereal vibes wafting down from up north. The guy hadn't died! If anything, this was a sign he was thriving. But his departure was a highly public, embarrassingly on-the-nose example of Canada's brain drain, the exodus of workers who seek opportunities better than the ones in the domestic aisle. Douglas made a popular pilgrimage south for pilot season, which takes place during Canadian TV's winter slowdown. But then, another twist: after six months of auditions, Douglas was burnt out and ready to come home. "I missed my community, my friends and family," he told the *Globe*. LA had felt too phony; too smoky and mirrored; too, dare I say, *American* for Joe Canadian, homegrown hero. Back home, Douglas enjoyed a modest TV career before taking on a high-profile radio hosting gig with *As It Happens*, a flagship property of the CBC, the national public broadcaster. From 2011 to 2019, Canadians could tune into the familiar sound of his voice and be reminded of exactly what they were.

So, a happy ending for Canada; arguably one for Joe, too, though his trajectory feels like less of a win and more like a tale told to keep wayward children in line. You might be better off coming to terms with your own curtailed potential and never trying for America, because it may be too risky for you to try at all. Hunger and raw talent may be strong enough to propel you across the border, but it takes more grit than that to keep you there. You may have disavowed the meaningless signifiers of Canadiana in both your person and your work, but your essential self has still been forged at the intersection of comparatively stable social and political institutions. Free health care. Better gun control. Less money and clout, sure, but also less competition. What if you uproot your life, head south, and discover, talent notwithstanding, that you're just too soft for it? The Molson commercial was a part of my childhood, but I never knew about the juicy twist or the preachy coda until I started working on this essay. We tell the story of Joe Canadian for the dual triumphs of reinvigorated nationalism and savvy marketing, but it turns out the lesser-known kicker is *be careful if you try to leave.*

This is the impulse I've worried about in myself—that a one-way ticket across the border might reveal some ineradicable contradiction between myself and the life I think I want. At various points over the last few years, I'd start to lay the groundwork, like sending out job applications, but a part of me would shrivel with relief when I never heard anything back. I earmarked the visa process as part of a nebulous long-term plan, but I didn't thrill at the notion of spending ten grand to be made miserable by paperwork—I'd already done that during every semester of law school—so I never took any more concrete steps than saying "I'll do it eventually." Working in Canadian journalism, I'd often hear other editors reference the mythical former colleagues who'd moved to New York—America, in this context, is always New York. My jealousy would swell or shrink according to superficial similarities and differences, like our respective ages, or what subject we'd done our degrees in, or the fact that we both wrote about culture in a country with too few outlets for publishing that kind of writing. But while they'd launched themselves into the open sky, I still had the security of always being able to see the ceiling. I liked the way it made me feel cozy, enclosed. Working in Canada, it is possible to keep the ceiling in your sights at all times, like a prison guard, but also a companion. It's possible you'll even grow tall enough to touch it, and maybe that's enough of an accomplishment. Maybe you're not meant to aspire to more than that. Maybe this is who you are.

In preparation for my monthlong New York trip, I skimmed Didion's "Goodbye to All That" in horror. Who would subject themselves to that city for life after a warning so clear? Sure, I was going to New York, but I wasn't going to *stay* there. I was familiar enough with the city to know that I liked it, but also enough to know that it terrified me. I'd milk that month and take some meetings, bring my connections back to Canada and bask in the cultural advantages of the United States with none of the prohibitive expense. The city and I would make our love work, long distance. I had it all figured out.

Something had shifted, though. The gears that kept me traveling along the track in front of me, the one that runs around the tiny pond, were starting to lock. There were things I didn't yet want to do, but was no longer content not to know. Before I left for my month in New York, the city I had no intention of relocating to, I had a lot of coffee meetings with Toronto-based writers and editors. I had no job in place for when I returned to Canada at the end of the summer, and I was trying to put out feelers. Tucked between very granular questions about their career trajectory, which were mostly there to show I'd done my research, I asked each of my interlocutors if they wished they'd gone to America. My sample wasn't representative, but the overwhelming answer was *of course*. I had no property, no kids? Then what the fuck was I doing still in Toronto? Only one person I asked said no, she'd never tried, and regretted nothing. Another person, who'd spent time in the United States, told me that I was never going to do any better than where I was—and added, with a specificity that smacked of premeditation, that I'd "probably never get published in *The New Yorker*." It turns out that in Canada, we are not so nice that we don't eat our own.

Maybe *this* is who we are. Obsessively patrolling the borders of our national story and yanking back anyone who looks like they might make it over the wall. I've been lucky to carve out niches in so many parts of the culture industry, where I could see the ceiling and know I was enclosed and truly like it. But there's also a frustration that comes with tending to various cogs of a national identity machine. The blaze of Canadian storytelling often burns away to the same dull refrain, whether you're turning down a magazine pitch about the country's hideous past for being too depressing, or flattening your rounded vowels in front of a mic so you don't distract an American cartoon viewer: *Is this who we are? Is this who we are? Is this who we are?*

AS A KID, I thought of the United States as merely Disney World and whatever states we had to drive through to get there, with occasional trips to Buffalo on weekends. Because I was a rule-abiding Canadian child, I understood the gravity of the moment at the border when my dad rolled down the rear window and I'd have to attest, on behalf of my siblings, that these were indeed my "real parents" (as a mixed family, they gave us so much shit, especially when my mom still carried her Trinidadian passport). The American picture began to fill out very slightly in adolescence—a forty-eight-hour stop in New York City to see *Wicked*, a day trip to DC to do some press for the animated show *Atomic Betty*, a short stint in Atlanta for the same. None of these stays were long enough to get the flavor of the place apart from brief, vivid impressions—New York was mostly Broadway, DC a phallic monument, Atlanta fried green tomatoes and crab hash. The only place I got proper repeat exposure to was Los Angeles, and after a few visits, I was ready to pledge my life to it.

When I was thirteen, I traveled to LA for the second time. Both that trip and the one before it had been for professional reasons—first to attend an award show for young actors (I didn't win), and then to sneak into the Grammy Awards on somebody's spare ticket (I *did* win, because I saw Green Day in person). Being in LA drew a bright line between my ideal future and the place where that fantasy might transmute into real life. California was where genuine artists lived. Where stars lived. Where *Green Day* lived. When my dad and I landed back in Toronto, I took the comedown hard. I felt like I'd been torn away from the root of my future, though I may have been confusing this with being torn away from Billie Joe Armstrong (not literally). I channeled my despair into song, my preferred medium at the time, and the thing I hoped to go to LA and get famous for. The song was titled, appropriately, "California."

The lyrics contain some vague references to sky and home and feeling "twisted," and the chorus ends on the phrase "destination unknown," which seems like a critical error in a piece meant as a love song to a specific place. As the architect of a dreamy California, I was neither precise nor accurate in what I built. The lack of geographic detail wasn't deliberate—my main experience of the city had been from the backseat of a car; my dad and I had spent a lot of time on freeways and not much of it in nature, and I was working with what I had. But the point wasn't to evoke a faithful California as much as to advance a clear thesis: America is the crucible of fortunes. I may not have known that much about the United States, but even at the time, I knew that this was true. I wonder, now, if the song was actually a four-minute subtweet at my parents, hoping they'd pick up on the intensity of my longing and realize it was unconscionable not to move our family there.

Years later, I'd set a novel in Toronto, but I still had my characters fly to New York City for the climactic action, because New York City felt like a more convincing setting for climactic action to take place. My characters arrived in New York and spent too many lines remarking on facets of its essential New York–ness, like the weird behaviors of pigeons and passersby. These images were mostly based on invention; I was twenty-two and it had been almost a decade since I'd seen the city at all. But I knew that New York was where you set your stories when you want them to be taken seriously, by American readers or otherwise. No one ever sat me down for a lecture about market size, but I'd intuited the principle in other ways, like being told to sound "more American" in studio—a staple of direction in Canadian cartoons. Or by arriving in LA, a known epicenter of creativity, and realizing that although I was a minor to moderate deal back at home, nobody there gave a shit who I was.

Canadian popular culture, especially TV, has a vexed relationship to place for similar reasons. The stakes of choosing a setting are more economic than aesthetic: base the story in the United States and maybe it'll resonate with its colossal audience. Base it in Canada, though, and you'll be eligible for certain grants and tax incentives (and also a pat on the head for helping consolidate the national character). For productions that justifiably want it both ways, the answer to *Whose house?* ends up being something like *Our . . . house?* This has happened enough times in TV that it's now a trope with a name: *Canada Does Not Exist*. A symptom of Canadian and cross-border productions, the trope involves a refusal to admit geographic specificity by muddling the indicators; a way to get the tax breaks but hopefully also lucrative syndication. In practice, this can look like what the late-eighties police drama *Night Heat* did—courtroom scenes bent their dialogue around red-flag terms like *district attorney* (we don't have those up here) or *Crown* (which is not what you call a prosecutor in the United States). According to the Canadian Radio-television and Telecommunications Commission (CRTC), the body that regulates broadcasting and ensures a certain percentage of domestic content, the bar to clear is whether the production is sufficiently "Canadian." But this isn't measured by the metrics, or the aesthetics, that the phrase *Canadian content* might immediately call to mind.

The CRTC has a noble mandate: to ensure that the material the population sees and hears "meets [their] needs and interests" by embodying values like equality, linguistic duality, and the "multicultural and multiracial nature of Canadian society." This is all very moral and high-flown, and implies that Canadians are a monolithic audience who only consume content of the highest rectitude. But embodying these values isn't what gets you the tax breaks. Behind the language of the Broadcasting Act, the CRTC has a much more granular set of criteria: a points system. Local director? Two points. Director of photography? One point. Lead performers? One point each. If the cast and crew meet certain quotas, and the production adheres to particular rules, it passes the test. (It can still fail others, though, most visibly the diversity one.) The points system is great for helping Canadian artists get work. But, while economically practical, it feels disconnected from the objectives of the Broadcasting Act. The combination of points system and highly moral legislation risks setting up a pretty major false equivalence: that, if enough Canadians are employed on a production, then it must express values that we all share. You know what passes this test with flying colors? The Molson ad. You know whose values it expresses? Not mine.

On the upside, you can shoot your show in Canada but set the story anywhere without pissing off the government. Or, if you're clever about it, without alienating an American *or* Canadian audience. Take *Schitt's Creek*, one of the most successful domestic exports of the past few years. The show follows the Rose family, whose astronomical wealth has been confiscated by an unspecified North American government, as they settle into the tiny backwater town of Schitt's Creek—their last remaining asset they bought as a joke years before. The CBC series spent a few seasons underperforming before Netflix acquired the streaming rights in 2017, which helped boost its popularity. In short order, the show was universally beloved by a cross-border audience except for a single sticking point: Where the hell was it set? As a CBC property filmed in small-town Ontario, Canada was heavily implied. But, as David Mack pointed out for BuzzFeed, "the show never really goes out of its way to highlight landmarks, flags, or political references that might give a viewer some context." Mack rounds up a series of screenshots from Twitter and Reddit, profiling an audience that is distinctly bothered by the imprecision. Was Schitt's Creek, the town, supposed to be in Canada? And was the Rose family meant to be Canadian or were they, as one Reddit user asked in a thread dissecting the question, "Americans forced to live in Schitt's Creek, Canada?"

Why did people need to know so badly? Did it deepen the degree of horror to think that the Rose family hadn't just fallen out of the 1 percent, but from the *American* 1 percent, and suffered the additional indignity of moving north? Would knowing whether the Roses were American help estimate their net worth (and is that useful intel for the viewers to calibrate their sympathies)? Would it helpfully recontextualize the family's early-season bitchiness—were these unusually nasty Canadians or just, like, normal Americans? Ditto the quirky residents of Schitt's Creek, the town—what kind of "backwater" are we dealing with, here? Do they have guns? Do they believe in diversity or assimilation; peacekeeping or policing? *Did these people vote for Trump?* While viewers were vocal about needing to know, nobody said why knowing would have made a difference. My suspicion is that there's a whole contextual framework by which Americans read Canadian cultural products—simply knowing something was produced up north brings with it a host of assumptions. If those expectations, like mainlining maple syrup, are not met, then this reads as a perceived mismatch between the form and the content. American viewers, in other words, are harder to please than the Canadian government. Canadians have come to expect this framework, too. It's how we're taught to evaluate the things that were made here. If it was done by one of our own, and *especially* if the Americans decide it's cool, then it ought to be veritably grubby with the fingerprints of Canadianness. This is why people like Drake so much, on both sides of the border. He plays right into this agenda by making the Great White North his entire persona.

What none of the *Schitt's Creek* fervor stops to contemplate is that the setting might have been kept vague on purpose, and that choice might have had something to do with the show's success. The series' creators, father-son team Eugene and Dan Levy, spent part of the press circuit committed to the Canada-does-not-exist bit. "There is no location for it," Eugene Levy said in a 2018 interview with Stephen Colbert. "There is no country. It is what it is." In an interview for David Mack's BuzzFeed piece, Dan Levy said that this placelessness was deliberate, a way to convey the depth of the Roses' isolation: "[T]he more people can recognize and identify [a location]," Levy told BuzzFeed, "the more that the focus gets shifted from 'Oh my god, we're stranded here and there's no way out' to 'I live near there and I actually know this place and this place and this place.'" In other words, people might have started claiming it as their own and putting their grubby fingerprints on it, though I don't think Levy means anything hostile toward hometown pride. But even though the vagueness was a deliberate artistic choice, the world still badgered it out of him: "I've never spoken about it, so I don't like to pinpoint it anywhere," Levy said, with palpable resignation. "But for the sake of the hard copy, I guess it's set in Canada." It was, after all, a Canadian show. (Personally, I had been so sure it was America!)

But that *still* doesn't answer the question of the Roses' nationality. In the finale (spoilers ahead) Johnny Rose, family patriarch, gets venture capitalist funding for a lucrative business expansion. His wife, Moira, lands a starring role in a soap opera reboot. Armed with fresh fortunes, the family decides to scatter between New York and LA. They express no apparent ties to any other place, Canada or elsewhere. Even within one of Canada's most beloved exports of the past few years, the definition of success is unambiguous. (As the credits rolled, Philip wondered, "What are they going to do about visas?") Twenty years after Joe Canadian, the country seemed less salty about the exodus; if anything, making it to America now seems an achievement worthy of celebration. But despite cross-border success, the show still gets looped into conversations about Canadian moral superiority. When *Schitt's Creek* swept the 2020 Emmy Awards during COVID-19 and the cast reunited under fluctuating public health rules, their togetherness was cited by fans on social media as "one more thing Canada [was] doing better" than the United States.

YOU'VE PROBABLY CLOCKED by now that moral superiority is kind of our thing. The trade-off for grinning through "Dead or Canadian" is getting to wave the flag of something like *Meanwhile in Canada*. The catchphrase offers its own rallying point for national identity and rests on the notion that, while endless storms roil down south, news from up here stays cute and quirky, producing headlines like "Hundreds lose internet service in northern BC after beaver chews through cable" (cbc.ca, April 2021). Don't get me wrong, it's still a way to make fun of Canada; moreover, I have to believe its embrace by Canadians is at least semi-ironic. But the set of stereotypes it calls upon are much more flattering. The United States pokes fun at its neighbors' enviable, slightly guileless stability; Canada plays the smug straight man who has ethnic friends and doesn't own a gun. We may be boring, but culture's liability is the news cycle's asset. Imagine, in the endless nightmare of the Trump years, the reprieve of opening your Twitter feed and seeing that the day's top story was, simply, "Beaver fucks with Wi-Fi."

The 2016 election provided an especially becoming foil for Canada, whose history of "maple-washing"—sweeping unsavory aspects of its history and culture, like settler colonialism and genocide against Indigenous peoples, under the rug—was widespread even before such a handy distraction. The night of November 8, the Immigration, Refugees and Citizenship Canada website buckled under a flood of users. A number of Canadian news outlets crowed that this was causal until it got fact-checked: as it turns out, there was a coinciding deadline for people *outside* the United States to obtain a mandatory travel document from the site. But even as world events bent in favor of the #MeanwhileInCanada hashtag, it hasn't been unanimously embraced. On Twitter, people have appended it to stories of racist violence, highlighting the falsehood on which the phrase rests. A popular parody website, *Walking Eagle News*, also offers an ongoing corrective. The site, run by Anishinaabe writer Tim Fontaine, often publishes satirical features on Canada's hypocritical treatment of Indigenous communities, with headlines including "RCMP struggle to balance reconciliation with brutal attacks on First Nations people" or "Woman whose ancestors stole entire continent suspects Indigenous person [of] shoplifting." But, despite the pushback, #MeanwhileInCanada has overwhelmingly been used by both individuals and media outlets to gild things like pictures of Justin Trudeau cuddling baby pandas—as if that photo depicted just a regular day in the blessed life we live up north.

The refrain has spawned a seven-figure-strong Facebook group, a popular Twitter feed, and a subreddit "dedicated to only the most Canadian of news," with recurring subjects including animals, nature, and nepotism—the latter a pervasive national theme that gets far less play than it ought to, or than the cutesy shit does. Before it was shuttered in 2021, *Huffington Post Canada* kept a running tag of "Meanwhile in Canada" stories dating back to 2013. The most recent piece in the archives tips the national taste for politeness toward dangerous sycophancy: "B.C. Woman Leaves Glowing 4.5-Star Review of Victoria-Area Jail." I'm not denying this is newsworthy—a person leaving winky emoji–speckled notes for cops absolutely deserves to be part of a public discussion, namely about who gets to confuse prison with an Airbnb versus who gets murdered by police—but it's irresponsible to tag it "Meanwhile in Canada," like it's an archetypal instance of our whole carceral system. In an interview with *Global News*, the local constable noted that people were calling this "one of the most Canadian things they had ever seen," elevating fluke into fable while ignoring actual data: according to a 2020 study of police use of force in Canada, 48 percent of people shot and killed were Indigenous and 20 percent were Black. Purely by the numbers, those deaths are likelier candidates for being one of the most Canadian things you've ever seen. Not to pick on *HuffPo*, but a surprising number of stories in their archive try to tell us who we are by being pro-police, including "Student's Dance-off with Cop Is the Best Thing You'll Watch Today" (low bar), "Saskatchewan Mountie Busts a Move at Powwow" (yikes), and—forgive me for even quoting it—"'Police Navidad': Vancouver Police Car Swarmed by Carollers." Meanwhile in Canada, all cops are besties. I know they're zany little news items and outlets need their content, but these fictions are dangerous. They suck up valuable attention at the expense of real problems, the severity of which get totally sidelined. Is *this* who we are? Really?

At the start of the pandemic, the hashtag and the stereotypes behind it began to take on a life-or-death cast. The Great White North, with its reputation for diligent rule-following and its comparatively progressive leadership, appeared to be born for this; to the south, an imperiled state sought places to bury the rising number of dead. Meanwhile, in Canada, people were still alive. It was a weird time for nationalism in general: it's been hip to be horny for the Canadian passport since 2016, but as travel shuttered in 2020, citizens' lust for their own papers reached bizarre new heights. The general outlook, in news and social media, felt bifurcated. Canadians were participants in the global outpouring of shock and despair, but the river sometimes swerved away into ungainly relief—sure, it was bad, but if you wanted to see *worse*, just turn on someone else's news. You got the sense that, if people had been allowed to gather, they might have staged a dramatic reading of the beer commercial. Literary critic Northrop Frye famously coined the term "garrison mentality" to describe the terror provoked by the vast, elemental menace of the Canadian wild. The sheer, unignorable force of it made survival a foundational theme of the national literary consciousness. Grim endurance of atmospheric horrors for the collective good, in other words, was extremely our shit.

During the first of Ontario's wave of incomplete shutdowns, I, like everyone, carved a path for my miserable little walk. Every day, I clocked a growing number of flags drooping from people's eaves. Nothing's ever really stirred in me at the sight of any flag, let alone "mine"—if anything, I suffer from flag aphasia and can only remember the ones capitalism has vomited onto a preponderance of T-shirts and key chains—but I realized the bright red maple leaf could finally make me feel something: distrust. Choosing to fly it now of all times seemed uncooperative and childish. What did people think it was going to protect them from? The threat we faced was on a global scale, not a national one; this unit of measurement seemed only to portend further disaster. (It did!) Eleven days earlier Philip and I had returned from New York again, sensing the breeze of a closing border at our heels. In the city you could feel things just starting to turn: the recoil of neighboring tables if you sneezed in a restaurant, ratty napkins clutched uselessly between palms and poles on the subway.

Philip and I had visited the city together a handful of times by then. He was the reason I started going back at all—a long weekend in New York was the first real trip we took after we got together, and we tried to go at least once a year after that. There'd been the monthlong stay in summer, then a weekend by myself for business meetings, and then the anxious trip in March of 2020. Whenever we crossed the border into the United States, one U.K. citizen and one Canadian one, he always had a harder time than I did. My childhood sense of duty for explaining mixed passports, useful as it was, had long deserted me; now, border security's naked derision for non–North American papers made me boil so much I couldn't talk for minutes after they grudgingly let us in. Philip wasn't fazed, but his postgraduate work permit was running out. When we got back from New York, stuck in Canada for the foreseeable future, we figured we might as well enter the tunnel of his permanent residency application.

I spent the first week or so of my month in New York overwhelmed and afraid. I held onto arbitrary signs of not being from there, like relying solely on Wi-Fi when Philip had the foresight to buy a SIM card and running into random subway stations every time I had to text him. He was properly trying the place on as a prospective future home; I was "just visiting." But the luxury of the month gave my feelings time to turn. A month was long enough to understand the difference between a place that makes you complacent and one that makes you feel contextualized, a backdrop that issues you a challenge and clarifies the stuff you're made of. A couple of weeks in, when I stopped getting lost on the subway and I'd met everyone at the office where I was working and I slowed down enough to feel the rustle and whir of ambition around me, I suddenly felt like a string of DNA somebody had sequenced.

In Toronto, where I've lived my whole life, the city's energy flows endlessly toward the impulse to win, to never stop working until you hit your head on the visible ceiling. Then, you work some more. New York has that vibe too, maybe even more so, but I feel like everyone's more self-aware about it. And, more importantly, there's no ceiling. You can try to dominate the world and touch the clouds, but the world is so vast it would obviously be foolish to try. Toronto does not have this reality check; if it did, we'd all live better and more balanced lives. The things I'd worried about—being too soft for New York, not being quite *enough* for it—were true. But in practice, that inevitability felt freeing. When I got back to Toronto, I understood in a new, tactile way that I might one day leave it. I didn't know if it would be New York or somewhere else, and I didn't even have a reason to leave yet. I just knew the possibility was there, a ghostly timeline I'd have to choose whether or not to step into. But I'd also come back from New York and gotten another contract in Toronto that turned by dumb luck into a media staff job, so that was that— the choice had been made for me.

Once the pandemic hit, the impulse to leave Toronto began to look both impossible and unoriginal anyway. Op-ed pages and real-estate sections and the degraded renaissance of the "leaving New York" essay told an unfolding tale of exodus from urban centers, but very few people were getting across the border. My coping method for any form of upheaval, no matter how minor, is to cultivate a mole-like tunnel vision and insist that everything else stay exactly the same. In this case, that looked like recommitting to Toronto, to which I felt I owed more than abandonment as soon as things got difficult (is this . . . *nationalism?*). Philip felt differently; as someone who's felt the pull toward both America and adventure longer and more intensely than I have, being suddenly held in place felt more like being trapped, and my sudden imitation of a mole person didn't help.

But, as the likelihood of leaving Canada anytime soon shrunk, I had too much time to doubt the impulse to leave at all. I don't come from a line of leavers, for one. My grandparents on one side and great-grandparents on the other picked their respective greater-Toronto-area suburbs to settle in. Later generations didn't try to reinvent the wheel. Maybe our bloodline had only a tiny thirst for adventure. Honestly, the older generations could have it. Since the pandemic started, I'd taken the same walk almost daily while listening to the same playlist (on shuffle, for *variety*) and only switched up the route when I had to, because I'd moved to the other end of the city. Also, it was a pandemic! I couldn't be held to the life changes I'd flirted with before I knew what the world was on the edge of. Obviously you fantasize about a life elsewhere when you learn you'll be stuck in your shitty one-bedroom apartment for a year or more. That's no state of mind on which to stake a future. The onset of a crisis invites the saying and dreaming of wild, irresponsible shit, not just goodbye to all that, but fuck it, too—its self-satisfaction and its provincialism and the tedious inferiority complex it still tries to make the stuff of punch lines; the ways it's always made you feel unwelcome and how it's never really wanted you to reach your full potential, only just as much as it can tolerate and no more. When the world's all gone to hell, of course you feel the urge to rebel against a place and ethos and set of institutions that have otherwise been working just fine. That doesn't mean you should actually *do* it. Now get back in line.

I GUESS I got tired of repressing my sense of possibility. The prospect of an indefinite horizon in Toronto began to feel like purgatory, but there was also nowhere else to go. In smaller towns outside Toronto, people slit each other's throats to score winning bids on houses barely cheaper than the ones that made them leave the city in the first place. We submitted Philip's permanent residency application. I forced him to look at apartments in cities I had no desire to live in and he had even less. On one of my anesthetic walks, I swerved south and glimpsed Lake Ontario in all its toxic, awful beauty, and was so overcome by the fear and want of leaving that I began to weep. Philip's permanent residency application got sent back many months later, on account of a missing signature. We went back to square one and sent it out again. I desperately wrote America cover letters. The U.S. government changed hands. A company based in New York wrote me back and, eventually, offered me a job and a viable path to living there. Americans were getting vaccinated and could, it seemed, begin to inhabit the fabled other side. Meanwhile, in Canada, the infection rate soared, the vaccine rollout stuttered. People remarked, with a maturity that struck me as a wasted chance to gloat, on the shock of turned tables (Dead *and* Canadian!). The situation had all the makings of a humbling epiphany, an opportunity to bring the national narrative to its knees and ask whether this relentless story of morality might actually be doing us harm. Later, of course, the two countries' fortunes reversed again, as Canada pulled ahead in vaccination rates and cases exponentially rose in the United States. If there was ever going to be an epiphany, we missed the window.

The same week as Canada was setting new precedents for COVID-19 case numbers, the U.S. News and World Report released its 2021 Best Countries rankings. As overall best in show, Canada was named top dog, dethroning Switzerland, the previous year's victor. Canada also swept the subcategories, taking the trophies for things like "quality of life" and "social purpose," as well as the more niche ones of "being viewed as not corrupt" and "respecting property rights." The project's methodology is iffy: based on a survey of twenty thousand people from across the world, it aggregates responses to rank countries on how they are perceived, rather than how they actually are as evidenced by statistics or policy. Old myths die hard: According to respondents who mostly don't live here, Canada is seen as "having a good job market, caring about human rights, and [being] committed to social justice." Several domestic outlets reported uncritically on the win. None of them stopped to ask whether we deserved it, or even to remark that maybe, given the number of people who were dying, the timing felt a little weird.

Meanwhile, in Canada, the remains of 215 children were unearthed from an unmarked grave in Kamloops, BC, at the site of a former residential school—the government-sponsored, church-run system that took Indigenous children from their families for the nominal purpose of giving them a Euro-Christian education, a negligible veil for cultural genocide, abuse, and mass murder. Hundreds of more burial sites were located in the weeks and months that followed. The unmarked graves were a reminder of Canada's ongoing failure to implement the calls to action in the Truth and Reconciliation Commission report. Back in 2009, the commission had requested $1.5 million to search for the children, but their ask was denied by the government. Mere days after the discovery, the *Globe and Mail* ran an op-ed on, among other things, how the *real* victims of colonialism in Canada had been white French Canadians. Right-wing op-eds have begun to say the quiet part loud, turning dog whistles into regular whistles, shrill and petulant. Centrist media had a crisis of conscience and had to overcorrect as questions of injustice abruptly became mainstream rather than niche. How many more examples that transgress the national fantasy do you need? Despite all the allegations of our niceness and our multiculturalism, despite the legacy of Joe Canadian, when it all comes down, this is who we are. Maybe what Canadians liked about old Joe all along was what he *didn't* say, and didn't have to. Maybe he professed to just enough of the right things that they believed, deep down, he was really one of them: Someone who can say a canned line about how much he values diversity but wouldn't hesitate to protest vaccine passports outside a hospital. Someone who thinks that, of all the victims in the checkered history of this country, the real one has always been him.

IN *CIVILIZATION AND its Discontents*, Freud writes of the "narcissism of minor differences," his term for the tiny antagonisms that simmer between bordering nations. Such rivalries, he says, are petty release valves for aggression, but also the glue that enables social cohesion. When it comes to Canada and the United States, this checks out, even as one wishes that Canada, when faced with an invitation to be narcissistic, had chosen a better hill to die on. I'm grateful to have been born here and to have called it home for so long (I keep saying *here, us, ours,* though by the time people read this, I don't know where I'll be and may have set out on my own American experiment): The fabled universal health care that doesn't cover dental and that my partner spent several years being unable to access until his permanent residency application went through. The national promise that diversity is our strength, a slogan with which my lived experience has always been in constant friction. We've had a good run, Canada and me. When the move to New York comes, I don't expect the leaving to be easy. But this accident of birth has never seemed synonymous, or even logically correlated, with believing in a set of principles that separate *us* from *them.* I was raised to pin a little maple leaf to my backpack when I traveled, to preemptively correct the assumption that I was from the Bad Place and make other people be the ones to say *sorry.* This, and no more, feels like the appropriate role for nationalism—a line edit, a correction, but never substantive enough to be elevated into thesis or theme.

I'm one of the lucky ones. Before the pandemic, "Dead or Canadian" was an abstraction, a warning of what my career might become rather than a description of my life's disposability in service of the economy. For a story of national virtue I thought I didn't buy into, the letdown has been rougher than expected. I guess there were still some illusions left to cut away. I'm not naïve enough to hold anyone, let alone incoherent entities like nations, to the punitive standard of upholding every single one of the values they profess. You have to pick your battles or the fight will burn you out. But oh, Canada. I'm so tired.

On that same trip to Nashville, before we flew to New York to make the leap that would rearrange my priorities and eventually my life, we dipped into Kentucky to explore the state's network of caves. As we drove across state lines, through thunderous rain and past improbably verdant hills, Lee Greenwood's "God Bless the U.S.A." came up on our host's playlist. It wasn't the first time I'd heard that song, but it was the first time I properly listened to it. It had the tinny ad-campaign taste of any piece of artistry that tries to balance aesthetic and nationalistic urges; a flavor I've been trained to recognize and encouraged to replicate. But, unlike the examples I'd been raised on, this bit of propaganda contemplated no *them*, just *us*. It conveyed a sense of pride so all-encompassing, there wasn't room for anybody else to exist, even hypothetically. I had the clammy sense that I was eavesdropping on somebody jerking off. But the song so obviously got its rocks off *knowing* that I overheard its pleasure, a reflexive vanity I almost had to respect. It only pulled me into deeper listening as I wondered what such shameless heights of self-love must feel like.

Acknowledgments

Thank you to my editors, Bhavna Chauhan, Julia Cheiffetz, and Melanie Tutino, for challenging me, championing my work, and trusting my vision.

Much gratitude to my agent, Rayhané Sanders, for shepherding me through the weird world of publishing with great care. When I first sent her a proposal for this book in 2019, she saw what it could be and helped shape what it became.

Amara Balan and Nick Ciani at One Signal Publishers were also generous, sharp readers. Thank you to James Iacobelli for taking my disorganized thoughts and turning them into the cover of my dreams, and to Carla Benton for delving so joyfully into the copy edit. I'm grateful to Milena Brown, Shida Carr, and Kaitlin Smith for spearheading this book's marketing and publicity. My thanks, more broadly, to the entire teams at One Signal/Atria and Doubleday Canada—in every interaction we had, I sensed such an affirming belief in this book.

Thanks to my former colleagues at *The Walrus*. Samia Madwar, Viviane Fairbank, and Erin Sylvester hired me and taught me how to fact-check, a skill set I drew on every time I sat down to work on this book. Eternal solidarity with my small but mighty digital team: Angela Misri, Natalie Vineberg, and Sheena Rossiter. Thank you to Daniel Viola for offering to cover my book leave, then sticking with the gig when I never came back. Lauren McKeon opened many doors for me but also helped me see when it was time to close them. Carmine Starnino, thanks for always having my back. Whenever I mused about going for it, whatever *it* was—a web project, a book, a job—the first thing you said was always, "Of course you should" and the second was, "How can I help?"

My friends and colleagues, past and present, at Catapult, especially Nicole Chung, Matt Ortile, Andy Hunter, Stella Cabot Wilson, Allisen Hae Ji Lichtenstein, Eliza Harris, Megha Majumdar, and Mensah Demary. Thank you for trusting me from the jump and for supporting my creativity on the job and off. Nicole, your mentorship has changed my life—I'm lucky to join the chorus of people who'd say the same. Thank you for hiring me and for supporting me at so many critical junctures.

Many thanks to the editors of earlier versions of some of these pieces: Rachel Sanders, Dana Snitzky, and Jess Zimmerman. Jess— you were the first person to take me seriously as an essayist, and at a time when I had no bylines or literary community to speak of, that meant everything. I'm grateful that you and Halimah Marcus trusted me to helm *Electric Literature* in the summer of 2019. To all the writers I've had the privilege to edit and all the ones yet to come: thank you. Your words nourish me and keep me going.

I'm so grateful to my generous early readers for taking the time to lend their support to this book: Saeed Jones, Kristen Arnett, Nicole Chung, Kamal Al-Solaylee, Jess Zimmerman, and Sarah Hagi.

Thank you to my mentors in undergrad and grad school who were patient and kind as I figured a lot of stuff out on the page: Anver Emon, Robert McGill, and Nick Mount.

Amy Brady, my brilliant friend and collaborator on the anthology *The World as We Knew It*—so much of this publishing journey is one we've been on together. I can't wait for your book.

Thank you to the family and friends who checked in and cheered me on: Ken and Helen Simon, Mel Isen, Mike and Mary Sayers, Ted Parker and Chiara Graf, Paul Coulter and Joanna Olivera, Mari Ruti, Pia Abrahams, Connie Campbell, and Amanda Bertucci. Thank you to Joe Neill and Kathryn Acord for their Nashville hospitality, and for letting me in on the secret of "Dead or Canadian." Sorry I got salty about it, but obviously I found it very useful.

My parents, who laid the foundations for all this. You taught me how to read, drove me all over the city to get me the *Redwall* books in the right order—I can trace a bright line from there to here—and have supported me in every pursuit, no matter how impractical. To my siblings, Nissae, Joshua, Koebe, and Bria-Jenée: Though this book is about my experiences, I hope I've managed to capture something that feels true to you, too. Nissae, your compassion and humor set an example I try to follow. A lot of these essays were informed by our conversations about life and work. I hope it makes you laugh.

Finally, my partner, Philip Sayers, without whom this book wouldn't exist. The roles of "first reader" and "ideal reader" seem like they'd be a conflict of interest, but you made it look (and feel) easy. Thank you for helping me think through every part of this project, for bending the shape of our life in support of it, and for working to create the conditions in which it's possible to write. This is ours.

Bibliography

Hearing Voices

Dobrow, Julie, Calvin Gidney, and Jennifer Burton. "Cartoons and
  Stereotypes." *The Conversation*, March 7, 2018. https://theconversation
  .com/why-its-so-important-for-kids-to-see-diverse-tv-and-movie
  -characters-92576.

Dobrow, Julie, Calvin Gidney, and Jennifer Burton. "Why It's So
  Important for Kids to See Diverse TV and Movie Characters." *The
  Conversation*, March 7, 2018. https://theconversation.com/why-its-so
  -important-for-kids-to-see-diverse-tv-and-movie-characters-92576.

Giorgis, Hannah. "What Does it Mean to 'Sound' Black?" *The Atlantic*,
  August 15, 2018. https://www.theatlantic.com/entertainment
  /archive/2018/08/what-does-it-mean-to-sound-black/567416/.

Hagi, Sarah. "All Your Favorite Cartoon Characters Are Black." *Vice*,
  April 21, 2017. https://www.vice.com/en/article/bme7bq/all-your
  -favourite-cartoon-characters-are-black.

Hartman, Saidiya V. *Scenes of Subjection: Terror, Slavery, and Self-Making in
  Nineteenth-Century America*. New York: Oxford University Press, 1997.

Hsu, Hua. "The Soft Racism of Apu from 'The Simpsons.'" *The New
  Yorker*, November 16, 2017. https://www.newyorker.com/culture
  /cultural-comment/the-soft-racism-of-apu-from-the-simpsons.

Jackson, Lauren Michele. "The Messy Politics of Black Voices—and
  'Black Voice'—in American Animation." *The New Yorker*, June 30,
  2020. https://www.newyorker.com/culture/cultural-comment/the
  -messy-politics-of-black-voices-and-black-voice-in-american
  -animation.

Johnson, Russo, Colleen, Adrianna Ruggiero, Kim Wilson, and Josanne
  Buchanan. "Examining Children's Animated Television in Canada

(2018/2019)." *Children's Media Lab*, January 7, 2021. https://drive
.google.com/file/d/1joJnhJLu8CTZ1dtTB6UPPqZdIKbd0wB0/view.

Kang, Inkoo. "Inside 'Big Mouth's' Big Change." *The Hollywood Reporter*,
December 7, 2020. https://www.hollywoodreporter.com/tv/tv-news
/inside-big-mouths-big-change-4101005/.

Kondabolu, Hari. *The Problem with Apu*. truTV, November 19, 2017.

Lehmann, Christopher P. *The Colored Cartoon: Black Presentation in American
Animated Short Films, 1907–1954*. Amherst: University of Massachusetts
Press, 2007.

Sammond, Nicholas. *The Birth of an Industry: Blackface Minstrelsy and the Rise
of American Animation*. Durham, NC: Duke University Press, 2015.

Smith, Stacy L., Mark Choueiti, Katherine Pieper, and Hannah Clark.
Increasing Inclusion in Amination. USC Annenberg Inclusion Initiative,
June 2019. https://assets.uscannenberg.org/docs/aii-inclusion
-animation-201906.pdf.

Tiny White People

Harbach, Chad, ed. *MFA vs. NYC: The Two Cultures of American Fiction*.
New York: Farrar, Straus and Giroux, 2014.

Hoby, Hermione. "Toni Morrison: 'I'm Writing for Black People. I Don't
Have to Apologise,'" *The Guardian*, April 25, 2015. https://www.the
guardian.com/books/2015/apr/25/toni-morrison-books-interview
-god-help-the-child.

Lutz, Garielle. "The Sentence Is a Lonely Place." *The Believer*, January 1,
2009. https://believermag.com/the-sentence-is-a-lonely-place/.

Morrison, Toni. *Playing in the Dark: Whiteness and the Literary Imagination*.
Cambridge, MA: Harvard University Press, 1992.

——. "The Site of Memory." In *The Source of Self-Regard: Selected Speeches,
Essays, and Meditations*, 233–45. New York: Knopf, 2019.

Nabokov, Vladimir. *Strong Opinions*. New York: McGraw-Hill, 1973.

Park Hong, Cathy. *Minor Feelings: An Asian American Reckoning*. New York:
One World, 2020.

Row, Jess. *White Flights: Race, Fiction, and the American Imagination*. Minneapolis, MN: Graywolf Press, 2019.

Salesses, Matthew. *Craft in the Real World: Rethinking Fiction Writing and
Workshopping*. New York: Catapult, 2021.

Vaye Watkins, Claire. "On Pandering." *Tin House*, November 23, 2015.
https://tinhouse.com/on-pandering/.

Diversity Hire

Ahmed, Sara. *On Being Included: Racism and Diversity in Institutional Life*. Durham, NC: Duke University Press, 2012.

Berrey, Ellen. *The Enigma of Diversity: The Language of Race and the Limits of Racial Justice*. Chicago: University of Chicago Press, 2015.

Hunt, Vivian, Dennis Layton, and Sara Prince. "Diversity Matters." *McKinsey & Company*, February 2, 2015. https://www.mckinsey.com/~/media/mckinsey/business%20functions/organization/our%20insights/why%20diversity%20matters/diversity%20matters.ashx.

Kennedy, Randall. *For Discrimination: Race, Affirmative Action, and the Law*. New York: Pantheon, 2013.

Menand, Louis. "The Changing Meaning of Affirmative Action." *The New Yorker*, January 13, 2020. https://www.newyorker.com/magazine/2020/01/20/have-we-outgrown-the-need-for-affirmative-action.

Pesce, Nicole Lyn. "Why Do We Like to Watch Shows about Workplace Drama?" *MarketWatch*, July 30, 2018. https://www.marketwatch.com/story/why-do-we-like-to-watch-shows-about-workplace-drama-2018-07-30-12883332.

Powell, Lewis. Memorandum. "Attack on American Free Enterprise System." August 23, 1971.

Regents of the University of California v. Bakke, 438 U.S. 265 (1978).

Urofsky, Melvin I. *The Affirmative Action Puzzle: A Living History from Reconstruction to Today*. New York: Pantheon Books, 2020.

This Time It's Personal

Barkhorn, Eleanor. "First Person, Vox's new section devoted to narrative essays, explained." *Vox*, June 13, 2015. https://www.vox.com/2015/6/12/8767221/vox-first-person-explained.

Bennett, Laura. "The First-Person Industrial Complex." *Slate*, September 14, 2015. http://www.slate.com/articles/life/technology/2015/09/the_first_person_industrial_complex_how_the_harrowing_personal_essay_took.html.

Bernstein, Arielle. "The 'Personal Essay Boom' Is Dead. Long Live the Personal Essay!" *Salon*, June 11, 2017. https://www.salon.com/2017/06/11/the-personal-essay-boom-is-dead-long-live-the-personal-essay/.

Bossiere, Zoë. "A Response to Jia Tolentino's 'The Personal-Essay Boom Is Over.'" *Brevity*, June 12, 2017. https://brevity.wordpress

.com/2017/06/12/a-response-to-jia-tolentinos-the-personal
-essay-boom-is-over/.

Brown, Stacia L. "The Personal Essay Economy Offers Fewer Rewards
for Black Women." *The New Republic*, September 18, 2015. https://
newrepublic.com/article/122845/personal-essay-economy-offers
-fewer-rewards-black-women.

Cheng, Anne Anlin. *The Melancholy of Race: Psychoanalysis, Assimilation, and
Hidden Grief*. New York: Oxford University Press, 2001.

Du Bois, W.E.B. *The Souls of Black Folk*. Brooklyn, NY: Restless Books,
2017.

Hurston, Zora Neale. "How It Feels to Be Colored Me." *The World
Tomorrow*, May 1928. https://www.casa-arts.org/cms/lib/PA01925203
/Centricity/Domain/50/Hurston%20How%20it%20Feels%20to%20
Be%20Colored%20Me.pdf.

Jefferson, Cord. "The Racism Beat." *Matter*, June 9, 2014. https://medium
.com/matter/the-racism-beat-6ff47f76cbb6.

Jerkins, Morgan. "How I Overcame My Anger As a Black Writer Online." *Lenny Letter*, August 1, 2017. https://www.lennyletter.com/story
/how-i-overcame-anger-as-a-black-writer-online.

Oyler, Lauren. "What Do We Mean When We Call Art 'Necessary'?"
The New York Times Magazine, May 8, 2018. https://www.nytimes
.com/2018/05/08/magazine/what-do-we-mean-when-we-call-art
-necessary.html.

Roberts, Soraya. "The Personal Essay Isn't Dead. It's Just No Longer
White." *The Walrus*, September 20, 2017. https://thewalrus.ca/the
-personal-essay-isnt-dead-its-just-no-longer-white/.

Spencer, Ruth. "The First-Person Essays Boom: Top Editors on Why
Confessional Writing Matters." *The Guardian*, September 15, 2015.
https://www.theguardian.com/media/2015/sep/15/first-person-essay
-confessional-writing-editors-writers?CMP=share_btn_tw.

Thorsen, Karen. *James Baldwin: The Price of the Ticket*. PBS, August 14, 1989.

Tolentino, Jia. "The Personal-Essay Boom Is Over." *The New Yorker*,
May 18, 2017. https://www.newyorker.com/culture/jia-tolentino
/the-personal-essay-boom-is-over.

Some of My Best Friends

Beck, Koa. *White Feminism*. New York: Atria Books, 2021.

Broder, Melissa. *So Sad Today: Personal Essays*. New York: Grand Central
Publishing, 2016.

Chotiner, Isaac. "Robin DiAngelo Wants White Progressives to Look Inward." *The New Yorker*, July 14, 2021. https://www.newyorker.com /news/q-and-a/robin-diangelo-wants-white-progressives-to-look -inward.

Dean, Michelle. *Sharp: The Women Who Made an Art of Having an Opinion*. New York: Grove Press, 2018.

Del Rey, Lana. Instagram caption. January 12, 2021.

Ephron, Nora. *I Feel Bad About My Neck: And Other Thoughts on Being a Woman*. New York: Vintage Books, 2006.

Farah, Safy Hallan. "All Alone in Their White Girl Pain." *Hip to Waste*, August 1, 2020. https://hiptowaste.substack.com/p/all-alone-in-their -white-girl-pain.

Frankenberg, Ruth. *White Women, Race Matters: The Social Construction of Whiteness*. Minneapolis: University of Minnesota Press, 1993.

Hamad, Ruby. *White Tears/Brown Scars: How Feminism Betrays Women of Color*. New York: Catapult, 2020.

Jamison, Leslie. "Grand Unified Theory of Female Pain." *VQR*, Spring 2014. https://www.vqronline.org/essays-articles/2014/04/grand -unified-theory-female-pain.

Meyers, Nancy, dir. *Something's Gotta Give*. Columbia Pictures, December 12, 2003.

Nelson, Deborah. *Tough Enough: Arbus, Arendt, Didion, McCarthy, Sontag, Weil*. Chicago: University of Chicago Press, 2017.

Orr, Niela. "White-Hot Furies." *The Baffler*, November 5, 2020. https:// thebaffler.com/bread-and-circuses/white-hot-furies-orr.

Sarkar, Ash. "'This Is How Money Acts': The Limitless Appeal of 'White Mess' TV." *Novara Media*, December 10, 2020. https://novaramedia .com/2020/12/10/this-is-how-money-acts-the-limitless-appeal-of -white-mess-tv/.

Sontag, Susan. *Illness As Metaphor*. New York: Picador, 1978.

Wilson, Lana. *Miss Americana*. Tremolo Productions. Netflix, January 31, 2020.

Zakaria, Rafia. *Against White Feminism: Notes on Disruption*. New York: W. W. Norton, 2021.

Barely Legal

Alexander, Michelle. *The New Jim Crow: Mass Incarceration in the Age of Color-blindness*. New York: The New Press, 2012.

Backhouse, Constance. "Gender and Race in the Construction of 'Legal

Professionalism': Historical Perspectives." October 2003. https://
papers.ssrn.com/sol3/papers.cfm?abstract_id=2273323.

Damte, Meaza. "A Space to Have Tough Conversations or Another
Cog in the Machine?" *UltraVires*, January 25, 2021. https://ultravires
.ca/2021/01/a-space-to-have-tough-conversations-or-another
-cog-in-the-machine/.

Harney, Stefano, and Fred Moten. *The Undercommons: Fugitive Planning and
Black Study*. Wivenhoe: Minor Compositions, 2013.

Leiper, Janet, Raj Anand, et al. "Working Together for Change: Strategies to Address Issues of Systemic Racism in the Legal Professions."
The Law Society of Upper Canada, December 2, 2016. http://lawsociety
ontario.azureedge.net/media/lso/media/legacy/pdf/w/working
-together-for-change-strategies-to-address-issues-of-systemic
-racism-in-the-legal-professions-final-report.pdf.

Shepherd, George B. "'No African-American Lawyers Allowed': The
Inefficient Racism of the ABA's Accreditation of Law Schools." *Journal
of Legal Education* 53, no. 1 (March 2003): 103–56.

Taylor, Keeanga-Yamahtta. *From #BlackLivesMatter to Black Liberation*. Chicago: Haymarket Books, 2016.

White Jr., Walter Hiawatha. "Tracing the Roots of the Civil Rights and
Social Justice Section." *American Bar Association*, July 1, 2015. https://
www.americanbar.org/groups/crsj/publications/human_rights_magazine
_home/2015—vol—41-/vol—41—no—3—-50th-anniversary-issue
/tracing-the-roots-of-the-civil-rights-and-social-justice-section/.

Whren v. United States, 517 U.S. 806 (1996).

Williams, Patricia J. *The Alchemy of Race and Rights: Diary of a Law Professor*.
Cambridge, MA: Harvard University Press, 1992.

What We Want and When We Want It

The Black National Economic Conference. "Black Manifesto." *New
York Review of Books*, July 10, 1969. https://www.nybooks.com
/articles/1969/07/10/black-manifesto/.

Chatterton Williams, Thomas, et al. "A Letter on Justice and Open Debate." *Harper's Magazine*, July 7, 2020. https://harpers.org/a-letter
-on-justice-and-open-debate/.

Dietrich, Adam, Varun Bajaj, and Kellan Marvin. *Concerned Student 1950*.
Field of Vision, March 21, 2016. https://fieldofvision.org/concerned
-student-1950.

Ferguson, Roderick A. *We Demand: The University and Student Protests*. Oakland: University of California Press, 2017.

Kelley, Robin D. G. *Freedom Dreams: The Black Radical Imagination*. Boston: Beacon Press, 2003.

——. "Black Study, Black Struggle." *Boston Review*, March 7, 2016. http:// bostonreview.net/forum/robin-d-g-kelley-black-study-black-struggle.

Odell, Jenny. *How to Do Nothing: Resisting the Attention Economy*: New York: Melville House, 2019.

Schulman, Sarah. *Conflict Is Not Abuse: Overstating Harm, Community Responsibility, and the Duty of Repair*. Vancouver, BC: Arsenal Pulp Press, 2016.

Scranton, William W. *The Report on the President's Commission on Campus Unrest*. President's Commission on Campus Unrest, September 26, 1970. https://files.eric.ed.gov/fulltext/ED083899.pdf.

Smith, Stacy L. "Hey, Hollywood: It's Time to Adopt the NFL's Rooney Rule—for Women (Guest Column)." *The Hollywood Reporter*, December 15, 2014. https://www.hollywoodreporter.com/news/general -news/hey-hollywood-time-adopt-nfls-754659/.

Do You Read Me

Deahl, Rachel. "Former Knopf Assistant Sells Publishing Novel in Seven Figure Deal." *Publishers Weekly*, February 21, 2020. https:// www.publishersweekly.com/pw/by-topic/industry-news/book -deals/article/82464-former-knopf-assistant-sells-publishing -novel-in-seven-figure-deal.html.

Greenidge, Kaitlyn. "Sex in the City." *VQR*, Summer 2020. https:// www.vqronline.org/fiction-criticism/2020/06/sex-city.

Grossman, Claire, Stephanie Young, and Julianna Spahr. "Who Gets to Be a Writer?" *Public Books*, April 15, 2021. https://www.publicbooks .org/who-gets-to-be-a-writer/.

Harris, Zakiya Dalila. *The Other Black Girl*. New York: Atria Books, 2021.

Hurston, Zora Neale. "What White Publishers Won't Print." *Negro Digest*, April 1950. https://pages.ucsd.edu/~bgoldfarb/cogn150s12 /reading/Hurston-What-White-Publishers-Wont-Print.pdf.

Ledbetter, James. "The Unbearable Whiteness of Publishing, Pt. 2." *The Village Voice*, August 1, 1995. https://www.villagevoice .com/2020/06/11/the-unbearable-whiteness-of-publishing-pt-2/.

Lee and Low Books. "Where Is the Diversity in Publishing? The 2019 Diversity Baseline Survey Results." *The Open Book Blog*, January 28,

2020. https://blog.leeandlow.com/2020/01/28/2019diversitybaseline survey/.

Leilani, Raven. *Luster*. New York: Farrar, Straus and Giroux, 2020.

Ma, Ling. *Severance*. New York: Farrar, Straus and Giroux, 2018.

Maher, John. "Workers Across Book Business Take Collective Action Against Racism." *Publishers Weekly*, June 8, 2020. https://www.publishersweekly.com/pw/by-topic/industry-news/publisher-news/article/83536-workers-across-industry-take-collective-action-against-racism.html.

Maher, John, Andrew Albanese, and Jim Milliot. "Justice Department Sues to Block Penguin Random House Acquisition of S&S." *Publishers Weekly*, November 2, 2021. https: www.publishersweekly.com/pw/by-topic/industry-news/publisher-news/article/87783-doj-sues-to-block-prh-acquisition-of-s-s.html.

McGrath, Laura B. "Comping White." *Los Angeles Review of Books*, January 21, 2019. https://lareviewofbooks.org/article/comping-white/.

Romero, Shelly, and Adriana M. Martínez Figueroa. "The Unbearable Whiteness of Publishing, Revisited." *Publishers Weekly*, January 29, 2021. https://www.publishersweekly.com/pw/by-topic/industry-news/publisher-news/article/85450-the-unbearable-whiteness-of-publishing-revisited.html.

Sinykin, Dan, and Edwin Roland. "Against Conglomeration." *Journal of Cultural Analytics* 6, no. 2 (April 2021). https://culturalanalytics.org/article/22331-against-conglomeration.

So, Richard Jean. *Redlining Culture: A Data History of Racial Inequality and Postwar Fiction*. New York: Columbia University Press, 2020.

Dead or Canadian

Freud, Sigmund. *Civilization and Its Discontents*. 1930. New York: W. W. Norton, 2010.

Mack, David. "We Finally Know Where 'Schitt's Creek' Is Set." *BuzzFeed*, August 14, 2018. https://www.buzzfeednews.com/article/davidmack/schitts-creek-us-canada-setting-location-dan-levy.